225 Tips and Sew Easy Lessons to Improve Your Quilting Skills

Best of Fons&Porter

# Tips&Techniques

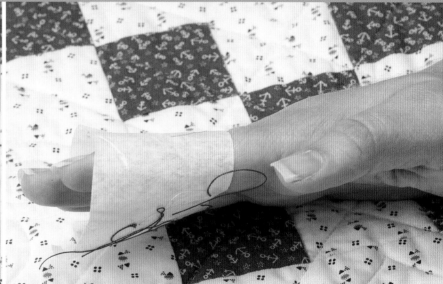

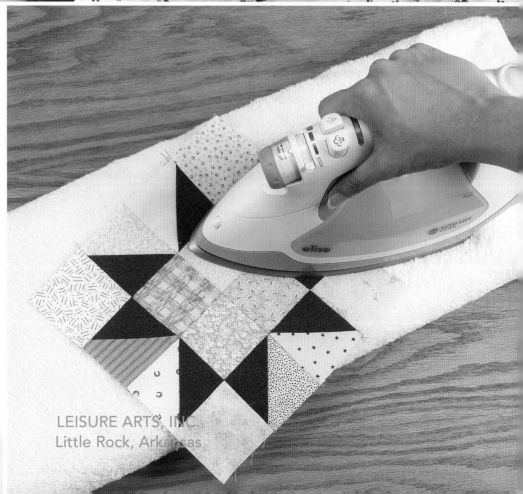

LEISURE ARTS, INC.
Little Rock, Arkansas

**FONS & PORTER STAFF**
**Editors-in-Chief** Marianne Fons and Liz Porter

**Editor** Jean Nolte
**Assistant Editor** Diane Tomlinson
**Managing Editor** Debra Finan
**Technical Writer** Kristine Peterson

**Art Director** Tony Jacobson

**Editorial Assistant** Mandy Couture
**Sewing Specialist** Cindy Hathaway

**Contributing Photographers** Dean Tanner, Katie Downey, Craig Anderson
**Contributing Photo Assistant** DeElda Wittmack

**Publisher** Kristi Loeffelholz
**Advertising Manager** Cristy Adamski
**Retail Manager** Sharon Hart
**Web Site Manager** Phillip Zacharias
**Customer Service Manager** Tiffiny Bond
**Fons & Porter Staff** Peggy Garner, Shelle Goodwin, Kimberly Romero,
Laura Saner, Yvonne Smith, Anne Welker, Karla Wesselmann

**New Track Media LLC**
**President and CEO** Stephen J. Kent
**Chief Financial Officer** Mark F. Arnett
**President, Book Publishing** W. Budge Wallis
**Vice President/Publishing Director** Joel P. Toner
**Vice President/Group Publisher** Tina Battock
**Vice President, Circulation** Nicole McGuire
**Vice President, Production** Barbara Schmitz
**Production Manager** Dominic M. Taormina
**Production Coordinator** Sarah Katz
**IT Manager** Denise Donnarumma
**Renewal and Billing Manager** Nekeya Dancy
**Online Subscriptions Manager** Jodi Lee

**Our Mission Statement**
Our goal is for you to enjoy making quilts as much as we do.

**LEISURE ARTS STAFF**
**Vice President of Editorial** Susan White Sullivan
**Special Projects Director** Susan Frantz Wiles
**Director of E-Commerce and Prepress Services** Mark Hawkins
**Imaging Technician** Stephanie Johnson
**Prepress Technician** Janie Marie Wright
**Manager of E-Commerce** Robert Young

**BUSINESS STAFF**
**President and Chief Executive Officer** Rick Barton
**Vice President of Sales** Mike Behar
**Vice President of Finance** Laticia Mull Dittrich
**Director of Corporate Planning** Anne Martin
**National Sales Director** Martha Adams
**Creative Services** Chaska Lucas
**Information Technology Director** Hermine Linz
**Controller** Francis Caple
**Vice President of Operations** Jim Dittrich
**Retail Customer Service Manager** Stan Raynor
**Vice President of Purchasing** Fred F. Pruss

Library of Congress Control Number: 2012937174
ISBN-13/EAN: 978-1-60900-376-0
10 9 8 7 6 5 4 3 2 1

We know that quilters are always looking for great tips to make their patchwork easier or more accurate. We're thrilled to bring you this collection of some of our favorite tips we've received from readers and TV viewers. They include ideas for organization of fabrics and tools, safety tips, and ways to use everyday items to help you with your quilting.

Our section of trademarked *Sew Easy* lessons will guide you via step-by-step photography through a variety of special techniques that will help you achieve more accurate patchwork. Also included is a section of quilt patterns that use the techniques covered in the *Sew Easy* lessons. There are quilts for all skill levels and in a variety of styles. Choose the one that's right for you and learn a new technique!

Happy quilting,

Marianne & Liz

80

86

66

120

112

124

# Tips

This section contains tips from the readers of Fons & Porter's *Love of Quilting*.

### Safe Storage

Use a potholder to make a case for scissors or rotary cutter. For a rotary cutter, fold potholder in half and stitch the side and bottom edges together. For scissors, bring two corners together and stitch edges. The loops can be used to hang cases in your sewing room.

*Maria Connan, Paris, Ontario*

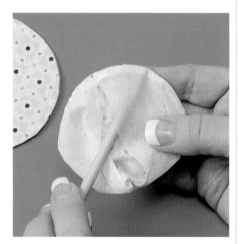

### Appliqué Turner

A knitting needle is perfect for turning appliqué pieces with fusible web on the back.

*Lorena Meza, Inglewood, CA*

### Safety Tip

*Always* wear shoes when using a rotary cutter. My rotary cutter fell off my cutting table, hit my bare foot, and landed on the floor. I ended up with ten stitches. Now, I always wear shoes when cutting.

*Deanna Hansen, Sioux City, IA*

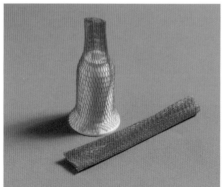

### Bud Nets

Ask your local florist to save the bud nets that protect flowers when they are shipped. The nets are great for keeping thread tidy. They are also good for holding stabilizer or rolls of wrapping paper.

*Karla Stimach, Katy, TX*

### Batting Scraps

When I have batting left from projects, I measure the pieces and pin a note to each one indicating its size. I store the pieces in a bag from that type of batting so I know what each is. When I need a piece for a project, I can easily see the sizes I have available.

*Grace Mitchell, Eagle River, AK*

## Curtain Tiebacks

My sewing machine is located in front of a window that has curtains for privacy at night. In the daytime, I like to let in as much sunlight as possible. I use large plastic hairclips to gather the curtains back on each side. When I am finished, my curtain falls back into place without wrinkles.

*Terry Harfner, Newtown Square, PA*

## Easy Quilt Hanger

For an inexpensive and easy-to-make quilt hanger for a wallhanging, buy large push pins and a dowel. Put the push pins into the wall, put the dowel through the hanging sleeve, and lay the dowel on top of the push pins. The hanging sleeve should be about 2" shorter than the dowel.

*Leona Pepin, Malone, NY*

## Extra Gift

When you make a quilt as a gift, make a pillowcase from the same fabrics and give it to the recipient. The pillowcase provides proper storage plus fabric for a patch if the quilt gets worn or torn.

*Kimberly Laderoute,*
*Lithia Springs, GA*

## Paper Plate Organizer

I recently made a quilt with 1,560 pieces and 195 blocks. To organize the project, I placed the pieces for each block on paper plate. I stacked up the paper plates, and as I completed each block, put the empty plate on the bottom of the stack. When I reached the bottom of my stack of plates, I knew that I had completed all of my blocks.

*Sally Mortenson, St. Paul, MN*

## Choosing a Stencil

When I go shopping for a quilting stencil, I take along a photocopy of a corner of my quilt. This way, I can try out different stencils in the store to see which one I like best.

*Barbara Braun*
*Brooklyn Center, MN*

## Wrap Up a Quilt

Wrapping quilts for gifts can be challenging. I purchased a laundry basket to put a quilt and matching pillow in, and bought a plastic tablecloth to wrap the basket. I tied the ends of the tablecloth in a large bow.

*Kathleen Cintavey, Olmsted, OH*

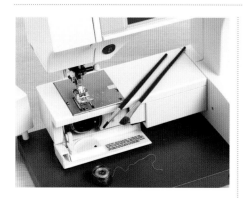

## Lint Brushes

Small paintbrushes come in handy to clean lint from the bobbin case area of your sewing machine.

*Lois Rasmussen, Sioux Falls, SD*

## Rotary Cutter ID

Attach a key chain with beads to your rotary cutter before you go to a class or retreat so you can easily identify your cutter. The chain is easily removed when you get home.

*Rosanne Panter, Elkhart, KS*

## Organizer Tray

I purchase ice cube trays at garage sales. They are perfect for arranging thread spools in sequence for embroidery machine designs. I use them to organize bobbins as well.

*Barbara Clark, Cedar Rapids, IA*

## Runaway Foot Control

At a quilting retreat, the foot control of my machine kept running away from me. I placed a floormat from my car under the foot control to keep it in place. It worked so well that several others did the same.

*Barb Spencer, Creston, IA*

## Sticky Situation

To remove residue on fabric left by fusible web, I clean the area with rubbing alcohol on a cotton ball. It removes the glue and dries clear.

*Wendy Kay, Castle Rock, CO*

## Time to Sew

When I sew, I use a digital cooking timer in my sewing room to keep me from losing track of time and sewing too long. This way, my family doesn't get neglected, and I'll be able to continue to quilt in the future with no complaints from my family!

*Karen Orlando, Stroudsburg, PA*

## Pattern Organizer

I use a three-ring binder and clear plastic sleeves to keep loose quilt patterns organized. When I watch quilting shows on TV, I jot down the instructions, type them later, and insert them into a sleeve in my book. My patterns are all protected, organized, and easy to see.

*Mary Sue Haag, Maxwell, NE*

## Filing System

I used to spend hours looking through back issues of magazines for a specific project. Now, I scan the front cover of each magazine and put the table of contents on the reverse side, highlighting projects I am interested in making. I store the pages in a binder, making projects easy to find later.

*Judi Blezek, Glenwood, IA*

## Cheer Up a Quilter

Instead of sending flowers to a quilting friend who is sick, give fat quarters or a gift certificate from her favorite quilt shop.

*Betty Orlando, New Lenox, IL*

## Multitasking Quilter

Cutting up old jeans for denim quilts is drudgery for me. To make this job manageable, I cut for half an hour during "Fons & Porter's Love of Quilting." Before too long, I have enough for a quilt, and the task is made easier by multitasking with something I enjoy.

*Delma Atwell, Boise, ID*

## Sweep Away Wrinkles

I layer my quilt on a clean floor, taping the backing, right side down, to the floor. After layering and before pinning, I take a clean broom and sweep the quilt! I start from the center and work my way out, sweeping from the center toward the edges. This gets all the wrinkles out of the batting and creates static electricity that helps keep the layers together.

*Kelly Whitaker, Rapid City, SD*

## Fabric Stiffener

When using spray starch to stiffen my fabric, I spray the fabric, place it in a plastic bag, and let it sit for ten minutes to absorb the starch. When pressing, I turn my iron temperature down a little to keep from scorching the fabric.

*Susan Isaacson, Tacoma, WA*

## Project Organizer

Use page protectors and zipper pouches to store information about your quilts. Put a page about the quilt and the quilter in the page protector; use the zipper pouch for photos of the quilt and pieces of the fabrics used. Store pages in a three-ring binder. If you want to show someone your project, don't take the whole book—just take the pages you need.

*Donna Zweifel, Beresford, SD*

## Fabric Shopper's Helper

When I take swatches of fabric to the quilt shop with me, I put them in a baseball card holder. Any divided protective sheet will work, but the baseball card holders are stronger than others. They keep the swatches flat, and I can put a note in the pocket showing what I need to purchase. The sheet folds up easily to fit in my purse.

*Connie Workoff, Bethlehem, PA*

## Tool Holder

To help me avoid losing my rotary cutter, seam ripper, or other tools in my sewing room, I hang a small basket on a hook meant to hold bananas. I keep it right next to my machine so my tools are handy.

*Laurette May, Fort Collins, CO*

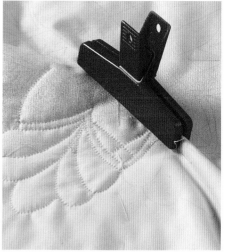

## Needle Protector

When I am hand quilting, I keep a large chip clip nearby. If I get called away, even for a few minutes, I place the clip over the section where I am stitching, making sure I cover the needle so no person (or pet) will get poked. The clip also helps me find my needle when I return.

*Susan Milliner, Cedar Park, TX*

## English Paper Piecing

A binder clip works well for English Paper Piecing Grandmother's Flower Garden units. The clip holds the hexagons together while I stitch.

*Julia Lier, Gladwin, MI*

## Medical Information

While at a quilt retreat, a new quilter to our group went into a diabetic coma. We didn't know her medical history, and the friend she came with wasn't there at the time. We wasted a lot of time trying to find the friend to get information. Now everyone who comes to our retreats fills out an index card listing an emergency contact person, medical issues, medicine they are taking, and any allergies. Each attendee puts her card under her sewing machine. No privacy is violated because no one looks at the cards unless there's an emergency.

*Mary Sue Davis Dayton, OH*

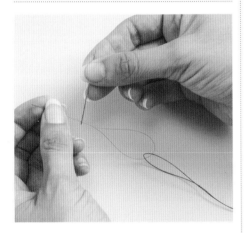

## Heavy-Duty Needle Threader

I use dental floss threaders to thread needles when I'm working with pearl cotton or embroidery floss.

*Betty Nail, Bolivar, MO*

## Cutting Mat Repair

My cutting mat warped when I left it in my car in the hot sun. To flatten it, I laid it on a towel on a table top and placed a hot, wet towel on top. I ironed the wet towel until it was dry, then flipped the mat over, wet the towel again, and ironed until dry. My mat was as good as new!

*Eva Cox, San Bernardino, CA*

## Mini Sewing Kit

A hard eyeglass case is great for storing a mini sewing kit. Insert a felt strip to hold needles and pins. Don't forget safety pins for little emergencies. Add a skinny spool of thread, a thimble, and a small pair of scissors.

*Linda Watson, Liberal, KS*

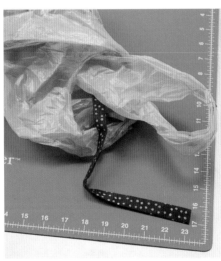

## Tangle-Free Binding

To keep my binding from falling on the floor as I am sewing it on, I put it in a plastic grocery bag. I pull one handle of the bag through the other and then slip the loop on my right arm. The bag is lightweight and now I don't step on the binding strip.

*Mary Schlagel, Phoenix, AZ*

## Block Storage

As I'm working on a quilt, I store my completed blocks in an unused pizza box.

*Georgianna Connor, Rindge, NH*

### Coasters

When I send a quilt out to be quilted, I always get extra fabric and batting back from the quilter. I use these scraps to make coasters.

*Judy Greer, Lebanon, TN*

### Tool ID Tags

Before going to quilting classes or retreats, I make ID tags to identify my tools. Using Ultrasuede, leather, or felt scraps, I rotary cut rectangles approximately 1" × 2" with a straight or decorative blade. I then punch a hole at one end and tie a narrow ribbon through it. I use a Pigma pen to write my name or initials on the tag, and then attach the tag through the hole in my tool.

*Cindi Blair-McManus, Lorton, VA*

### Stencil Organizer

Over the years, I have collected many stencils. To make a record of them, I purchased a sketchbook and traced each stencil in it. Now, I can easily look through the book to decide which stencil I want to use.

*June Brotherton, Dunkirk, MD*

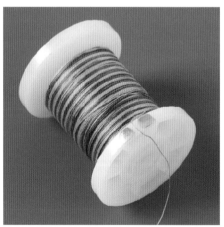

### Mark Your Spools

Use nail polish to mark the spot on a thread spool where the cut that holds the thread tail is located. You can then see the slot easily to thread the tail back!

*Judy A. Rose, Hockley, TX*

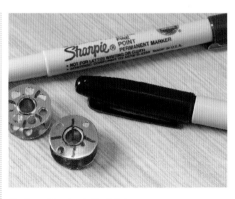

### Color Coded Bobbins

I have 5 sewing machines that use different bobbins. To avoid confusion, I color coded the bobbins with markers so I know which bobbins fit each machine.

*Pat Childress, Chesterfield, VA*

## Stress Reliever

To help with those days in the office when the stress gets to be just a little too much, I keep a few 4" squares of my favorite fabric on my desk, just to feel it. It's amazing what the feel of fabric can do for a quilter who would rather be home sewing than coping with the stresses at work!

*Teresa Childers, Orlando, OK*

## Practice for New Quilters

When I finish a quilt, I put leftover blocks into a plastic zip bag with the instructions and extra fabric. I label the bag "Practice Kit." I give these kits to my 12-year-old granddaughter or daughters and granddaughters of my friends. They enjoy the practice and are becoming more interested in quilting.

*Marcie Vitopil, Hilltop Lakes, TX*

## Organizer

I purchased a large mesh pencil holder to use on my sewing table. It keeps all of my tools close at hand, and keeps my sewing table neat.

*Teresa Courtright, Elmwood, IL*

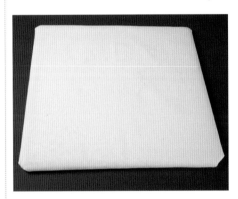

## Portable Ironing Surface

Make a portable ironing surface from a fireproof gypsum ceiling tile. Cover one side with a layer of cotton batting and then wrap cotton duck cloth around the board. Fasten the fabric with glue or double-sided carpet tape. This makes a handy lightweight board to carry to workshops or to use on your cutting table.

*Jan Dawes, Lakeview, AR*

## Eco Friendly Gift Bag

I use cloth grocery bags to wrap quilts that I make for gifts. I tie ribbons and bows to the handles and stuff in some tissue paper to make a pretty package.

*Cynthia Pugh, Laureldale, PA*

## Pressing Seams

When I only have a little pressing to do, I use half of a spring-loaded clothespin to press seams while I'm sitting at my sewing machine.

*Rose Pryor, Leesburg, VA*

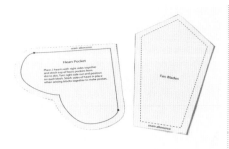

## Sturdy Templates

I laminate templates to make them sturdier so they last longer. I use contact paper or take the pattern to a copy shop to be laminated. Also, using card stock for the templates gives them extra strength.

*Darlene Sevin, Williamsport, PA*

## Protection From Burns

Wear a leather thimble on the index finger of the hand you use to hold fabric while pressing. The leather protects your finger from being burned by the steam. Be sure it's a leather thimble that does not have the metal disk in the tip!

*Peggy Quartermans, Blacksburg, VA*

## Homemade Note Cards

Apply fusible web to a favorite fabric and cut out a motif. Adhere the motif to a plain note card, and add some "stitches" with a fine-point marker if you like. You can make cards for holidays and birthdays, or just for notes.

*Karla Shaw, Mainesburg, PA*

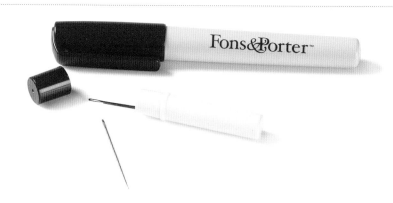

## Needle Case

An empty glue cartridge from the Fons & Porter Glue Stick is the perfect container for disposing of used needles. You can also clean it out well and use it as a needle case. The lid fits tightly, so it won't come open in your sewing kit.

*Bev Sheeley, Boise, ID*

## Rotary Cutter Holder

I found this calculator pouch in an office supply store. It's perfect for storing my rotary cutter when I go on retreats. It has a hanger on the back for convenient storage at home.

*Pam Broe, Little Meadows, PA*

## Scant ¼" Seam

When a pattern calls for a scant ¼" seam, I move the needle position slightly to the right. Even though I have the straight stitch throat plate on my machine, the needle still goes through the hole without any problem and makes a perfect width seam. I can still use the ¼" foot, too! (Be sure to test this on your machine before sewing to avoid breaking a needle or damaging your presser foot.)

*Lynn Schiefelbein, Sioux Falls, SD*

## Thread Keeper

A strip of Glad® Press'n Seal™ wrapped around a spool of thread will keep the thread from unwinding. Be sure to turn under about ¼" at the end so it can be easily removed.

*Kathy Hartgrave, Cedar Rapids, IA*

## Skewer Stiletto

I have found that a bamboo skewer works great as a stiletto. It is lightweight, inexpensive, and easy to hold. Take some to classes and retreats as favors for the other participants.

*Marylu Doyle, Princeton, IL*

## Thread Catcher

Set a coffee filter on your sewing table to catch loose thread ends.
You can even tip or drop it, and the thread stays on.

*Delores Moe, Dell Rapids, SD*

## Fabric Scans

When collecting fabrics for a project, I scan those that I have purchased and note where I got them and how much of each I have. I take the printouts with me when I shop so I know what I already have for the project.

*Dee Kilroy, Euclid, OH*

## No Lost Patterns

When I buy a quilt pattern and don't purchase the fabric at the same time, I make a color copy of the quilt picture and print the materials list on the back. When I am ready to purchase fabric, I take the copy to the store, eliminating the risk of losing the real pattern. A folded copy fits nicely in my purse.

*Linda Madsen, Pocahontas, IA*

## Rotary Ruler Handle

To make a handle for your rotary cutting ruler, purchase a woodworking push block. Use double-sided carpet tape to attach the handle to your ruler. If desired, attach dots of sandpaper to bottom of ruler to keep it from slipping.

*Maralyn Maxfield, Pulaski, TN*

## Tie a Quilt

A quick way to finish a quilt is to tie it from the back side. Use embroidery floss that matches the front. After tying, bury the threads in the batting for a cleaner look.

*Eleanor Mazourek, Neillsville, WI*

## Instruction Saver

If you have paper instructions that you need to preserve, use clear book cover adhesive plastic to seal both front and back. You can also protect pattern covers this way.

*Paula King, Clinton, OK*

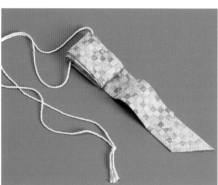

## No-Tangle Binding

To keep quilt binding from tangling, roll it up and put a shoestring or heavy cord through the center. Tie a knot in the cord and put it around your neck. Binding will feed nicely off the roll as you attach it to your quilt.

*Janet Hardin, West Alexandria, OH*

## Fabric Storage

I store fabric in a closet shoe bag. You can hang it over the back of a door for out-of-the-way storage.

*Joyce Pattison, Dallas, OR*

## Two at a Time

Like lots of quilters, I give many quilts away. Because it is sometimes hard to part with them, I now make two quilts at the same time—one to give away and one to keep. I do all of the cutting and piecing at once so I don't feel as if I am starting over to make the second one.

*Pat Braun, Princeton, MN*

## Keep Tools Handy

Wrap a rubber band around the handle of a tool that rolls such as a seam ripper or marking pencil. The rubber band also elevates the end of the tool just enough so that it is easy to pick up.

*Suzanne Yerks, Wingdale, NY*

## Iron Safety

Because he knows I sometimes forget to turn off my iron, my grandson made me a beaded bracelet to wear when I turn the iron on. If the bracelet is still on my wrist when I get ready to leave my sewing room, I know I need to check the iron. When I turn off the iron, I take the bracelet off.

*Linda Watson, Liberal, KS*

## No More Tangled Thread

To keep thread neat in your storage area, wrap a piece of clear lightweight vinyl around each spool to prevent tangling. You can buy the vinyl in fabric stores. Love your show!

*Mary Rubrake, South Whitley, IN*

## Machine Quilting Practice

Patchwork bandanas, which are inexpensive at craft stores, make great practice pieces for machine quilting. I find these especially helpful for beginners to learn quilting in the ditch.

*JoAnn Jeffries, Louisville, KY*

## Wrinkled Batting

To remove the wrinkles and folds from batting, I fluff it in the dryer for a few minutes on low heat or air only.

*Mary Tufte, Sioux Falls, SD*

## No-Slip Rulers

To keep rulers from slipping on fabric when cutting, brush a thin, small spot of rubber cement on the back of the ruler in several places. If you want to remove the rubber cement later, rub the spot, and the cement will ball up and come off.

*Peggy Steiner, Kent, WA*

## Machine Oiling Trick

Whenever I am going to be gone on a trip for an extended period of time, I oil my machine before leaving. That gives the oil a longer time to soak into the parts. When I return, I clean the residue!

*A.L. Jennings, Beckley, WV*

## Pencil Storage

I store my sharpened marking pencils in a toothbrush travel container to protect their points.

*Virginia Templeton, DeWitt, IA*

### Rotary Cutter Keeper

I keep my rotary cutter in a brightly colored slipper sock so it's always easy to find.

*Arlene Beavan, Tinley Park, IL*

### Thread Spools and Bobbins

When you buy sweaters or blouses, they sometimes come with extra buttons enclosed in little plastic bags. I use the bags to store a spool of thread and its matching bobbin. They're great for take-along projects.

*Sandra Griswold, Taylor, TX*

### Triangle Trimmers

I found that when joining bias strips for appliqué or binding, if I trim the corners of the longest sides, the ends are much easier to align.

*Ginger Patano, Spokane, WA*

### Choosing Fabrics for Quilts

When my family or friends ask me to make a quilt, I ask them to select paint swatches that match their décor. I use these to help me choose fabrics that complement their home.

*Catherine VanOrden,*
*Pawleys Island, SC*

### Reading While Quilting

I love to read and to quilt, but sometimes I don't want to choose between the two. To solve this dilemma, I listen to books on tape while I sew!

*Eleanore Brown, Champaign, IL*

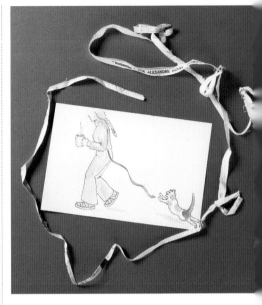

### Cats and Quilters

When I cut the selvages off my fabric, I tie the ends together to make a long streamer and tuck one end into my waistband. When I get up to stretch, my cat plays with the "toy" I drag through the house.

*Marcia Lietzau, Buffalo Lake, MN*

### First Aid for Books

One of my favorite quilt books was coming apart, so I took it to an office supply store and had them install a spiral spine to keep it together. This is an inexpensive way to save your well-used books.

*Patti McKee, Port Eglin,*
*Ontario Canada*

## Tool Organizer

I use a silverware caddy for the tools that I use while sewing. This keeps them organized and close at hand. When I'm done sewing, I put the tray in a drawer, leaving a tidy sewing room.

*Janet Amos, Grand Rapids, MI*

## Quilt Designs

As a new machine quilter, I'm sometimes at a loss when it comes to choosing quilting designs. I take pictures of quilts I like (with the owner's permission, of course), and put them in a small photo album. I refer to the album for ideas and inspiration.

*Nannette Konstant, Flourtown, PA*

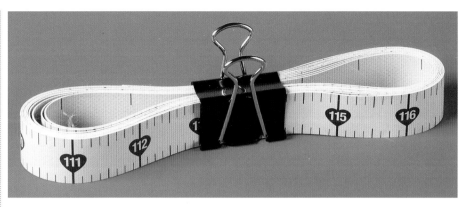

## Storage for Tape Measure

To keep my tape measure from coming unrolled, I put a binder clip on it. It also works as a hanger to hang the tape measure with other tools.

*Ann Ott, Wheatland, IA*

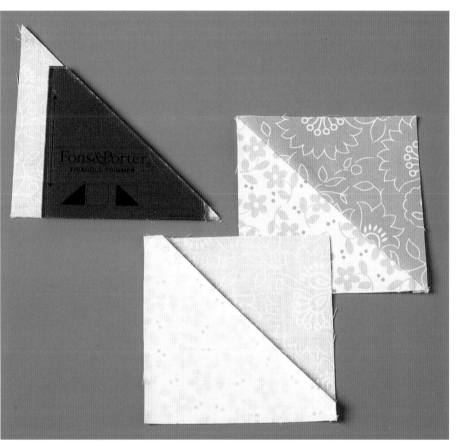

## Triangle Trimmers

I use the pink triangle trimmer when making triangle-squares. After pressing the sewn triangles flat, I use the triangle trimmer and trim off the points before pressing the square open. It's easier than pressing first then trimming off the dog ears.

*Lyn Makela, Half Moon Bay, CA*

## Pattern Storage

I use an expanding file for my appliqué patterns. Filing them alphabetically helps me to quickly find the one I'm looking for.

*Dana Nyklicek, Ontario, Canada*

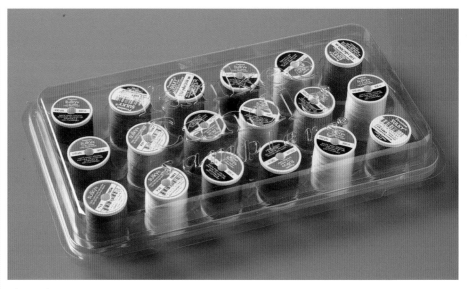

## Thread Box

Some stores give these plastic boxes away when you buy votive candles. They're the perfect size for holding thread, and they keep thread dust and tangle free.

*Marti Tourville, South Hero, VT*

## Pin Holder

I use travel soap containers for my straight pins and safety pins. They fit in my small tote bag for my quilting and they stay tightly closed until I need the pins.

*Dawn Cherni, Cleveland, OH*

## Tip from a Smart Kid

*Katie Larson, Kansas City, MO, suggested this tip when she was a young girl shopping with her mother:*

*If you're going to the quilt store with your mom, be sure to take a book to read. She's going to be there for awhile.*

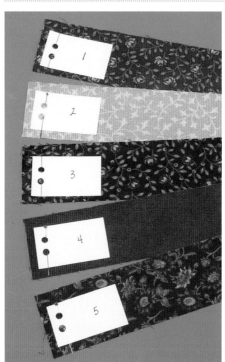

## Marking Rows

I cut index cards into quarters and punch two holes in each quarter. Then I number them with a dark marker. They are easy to pin to blocks or rows to keep them in the proper order when sewing together.

*Joyce Wallace, Mesa, AZ*

## Use Your Noodle

I use foam pool noodles to roll quilts for storage. They are about 2¾" in diameter and almost 60" long. The ones with a hole through the center can be joined with a ⅝"-diameter dowel to make a longer roller. To keep your quilt from touching the styrofoam, make a fabric slipcover for the noodle.

*Barb Jardee, Tucson, AZ*

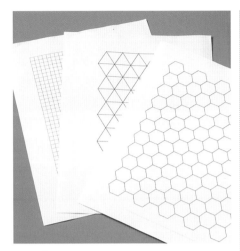

### Graph Paper

After searching several stores for the right graph paper, I discovered you can print free graph paper online. Search for graph paper, and you'll find several sites where you can choose design, size, line weight, and other options. You could print shapes for English Paper Piecing on card stock. Problem solved!

*Cally Hayden, Homestead, FL*

### Catch Thread Snips

Use a small square of batting when sewing or quilting to catch your thread snips. When it is full, clean it off or just throw it away. I find I have fewer threads on me and my quilts when I use this trick.

*Susan Miller, Cary, NC*

### Label Your Stabilizer

Different types of stabilizer look and feel the same. Use a pen to write the type on each piece so you won't get them confused.

*Mary Kirschenman, Yankton, SD*

### Binding Clips

I don't like using pins when hand stitching my binding so I use plastic coated paper clips. They are easy to slip on, and the thread will not get caught on them.

*Doris Parkes, Lexington, MO*

### Block Hanger

I use a skirt hanger to store my completed blocks. The clips can be moved to accommodate any size block. This keeps the blocks organized with no wrinkles.

*Nancy Shartle, Dayton, OH*

## Scrap Bag

Use a zipper sandwich bag to catch threads and small scraps while you are sewing. To keep the bag from closing, turn it inside out, and it will stay permanently open. You can tape it to your sewing machine or table.

*Jo Ann Jeffries, Louisville, KY*

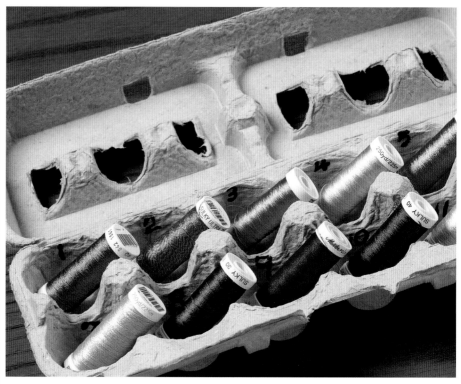

## Handy Thread Organizer

When using my embroidery machine to sew a multi-colored design, I select all of my threads before starting to stitch. I use an egg carton to hold the spools while I stitch the embroidery. I number the sections of the egg carton with the thread sequence numbers and place the spools in the carton in the correct order. After stitching, I replace each spool so I can repeat the design if necessary.

*Barbara Bedell, Liverpool, NY*

## Safety Reminder

Whenever I plug in my craft iron, stencil burner, or jewel wand to preheat, I slip a large, bright-colored ponytail elastic on my wrist. If I am called away by the phone, someone at my door, or some other distraction, the band on my wrist reminds me that my tools are on and require my immediate return.

*Brenda Beckstrom, Provo, UT*

## Stabilizer Solution

I like to use water-soluble stabilizer on a roll for embroidery projects, but found it difficult to find the end of the roll. Now, I cut the stabilizer with pinking shears so the edge is jagged and much easier to find.

*Kristen Corley, Cedar Park, TX*

## Copies on Fusible Web

When I need many pieces for a fusible appliqué project, I copy them with my printer/scanner/copier. I cut pieces of fusible web 8½" × 11" and print the pieces on the paper side of the fusible web.

*Jayne Reuer, Aberdeen, SD*

## Quick Reference

When I see a magazine pattern or article that I may want to use at a later date, I photocopy the first page, making sure the month, year, and page number are visible on the copy. I keep the photocopied pages in an indexed binder.

*Jean Engle, Pella, IA*

## Magnetic Bowl

At an auto parts store, I purchased a magnetic metal bowl designed to keep nuts and bolts from rolling away. It makes a terrific magnetic pincushion. When I spill my pins or needles, I use the magnet to quickly pick them up.

*Mary Rubrake, South Whitley, IN*

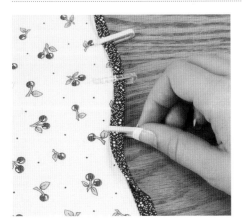

## Dry Cleaner Clips

While stitching my binding, I like to hold it in place with small plastic clips from the dry cleaner. They are free and work great, especially on small projects!

*Virginia Anderson, Shoreline, WA*

## Binding Hint

When hand stitching binding on a quilt, I stop every 10"–12", make a small knot, and then continue stitching. If the thread wears out or breaks, I only need to restitch a small section.

*Dolores Jarrett, Rapid City, SD*

## Hand Basting a Quilt

When I'm ready to baste a quilt, I tape the backing to the floor, then the batting, and finally the quilt top. I slip a marble under the quilt to create a bump so it's easy to stitch through the quilt without scratching the floor. I roll the marble to wherever I want to baste.

*Diana St-Coeur, Stymiest,*
*New Brunswick, Canada*

## Use Batting Scraps

Here's a way to piece leftover batting scraps to use in quilts. Overlap two pieces of batting about 2". Use a long ruler to cut through both layers so they have straight edges. Throw away the waste strips. Cut fusible interfacing into 2"-wide strips. Place interfacing atop the freshly cut batting edges and gently fuse in place using a dry iron. With batting side up, stitch together with a wide zigzag stitch.

*Amy Leonard, Des Moines, IA*

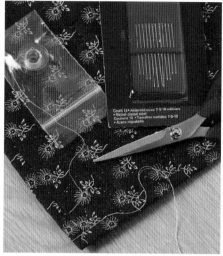

## Sewing to Go

When I carry a hand sewing project with me, I wind the thread on bobbins to save space, particularly if I need to carry a number of different colors of thread. To keep bobbins from unwinding and tangling, I put each bobbin in a plastic crafts bag and let the thread end extend a short way out of the opening. It is very easy to pull out the length of thread I need and cut it off, and the thread stays clean.

*Mary Lauer, North Platte, NE*

## Quick Quilt Hanger

To display a small quilted wallhanging, I use a twisted cord drapery tie-back and a wooden dowel. The tie-back has nice loops on both ends for the dowel and looks attractive.

*Sandi Collins, South Bend, IN*

## Project Organizer

I am a new quilter and am making my first Log Cabin quilt. I attached my cut strips to a pant hanger that had two clips on it. I used clothespins for the rest of the strips. I covered the hanger with a plastic bag and hung it on the back of a door to store my quilt in progress until I had time to return to my project. This worked great to keep everything neatly arranged.

*Char Reeves, Tucson, AZ*

## Pattern Saver

I laminate the pages of books or patterns I will use again and again. I use a dry-erase pen to mark each step as I cut and stitch. The marks can be "erased" for the next time I make the project.

*Kim Devine, Cumming, IA*

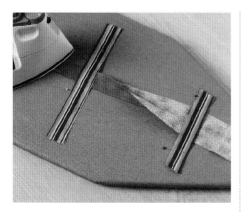

## Easy Folded Binding

When making folded binding, I always have a hard time keeping it from slipping off the ironing board as I press it. To solve this problem, I pin a small strip of cloth to the pointed end of the board, leaving enough space for the flat, unpressed width of the binding to pass through. On the other end of the board, I pin another small strip of cloth, leaving enough space for the folded part of the binding to pass through. I can press the binding while the fabric strips hold it all in place until I reach the end.

*Linda Binns, Oskaloosa, IA*

## No-slip Fingertips

I use Sortkwik, a tacky fingertip moistener, to pick up fabric pieces as I sew them together. It won't stain, and is just sticky enough to help pick up fabric easily.

*Glenna Kohlmeyer, Muscatine, IA*

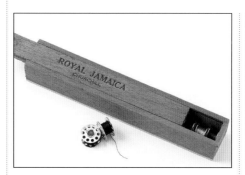

## Bobbin Storage

Use a cigar box to store bobbins. Some larger cigar boxes have inserts in them that make a perfect tray for bobbins.

*Shirley Allen, Roseville, MI*

## Marking Quilt Designs

If your quilt needs an additional small quilt design after it's been layered, cut a design from contact paper and press it in place on the quilt. Then, stitch around the shape either by hand or machine.

*Danis Hedrick, Sully, IA*

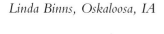

## Pin Holder

A magnetic paper clip holder works great for holding pins. The holders are available at office supply stores.

*Barbara Mueller, Chicago, IL*

## Handy Tool Storage

I keep my scissors and rotary cutters in potholders, which I hang under my work station. My tools are always handy while I am sewing.

*Robert Gaudreau, Garrison, NY*

### Ruler Rack

A folder rack from an office supply store is perfect for holding rulers. Place rulers in the rack with largest in back and smallest in front, it's easy to find the one you need.

*Maxine Kane,*
*New Albany, PA*

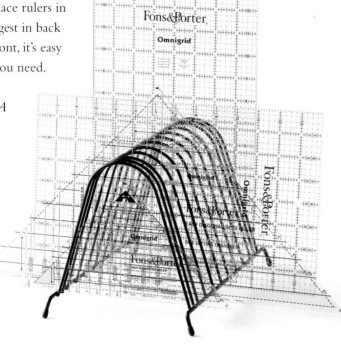

### Shopping Bags

I use leftover blocks to decorate shopping bags. The bags are much more fun to use this way, so I'm more likely to remember to take them along to the store. I also give them to my quilt friends as gifts.

*Kathy Myres, Moville, IA*

### Non-slip Templates

When using plastic templates, I find it helpful to spray temporary adhesive on the back. The template stays firmly on the fabric while I draw or cut around it, but it moves easily to be used again and again. When I'm done, I remove the sticky residue from the template with a product such as Goo Gone.

*Amy Gill, Bartow, FL*

### Numbering Rows

Use purchased beads with numbers to keep track of your quilt rows. Slip the beads onto medium-size safety pins, and attach them to the first block in each row. Leave the pins in until all rows are sewn together.

*Pat Lambert, Montrose, CO*

### Needle Storage

Use business card pages from an office supply store to hold needle cases. It's easy to find the needle you're looking for with these clear pages. You can also see at a glance which sizes you have and which ones you need to buy.

*Claire Gimber, Scottsdale, AZ*

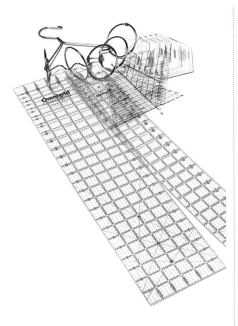

## Template and Ruler Hanger

The best way I have found to keep my templates and rulers within reach is a belt hanger. You can usually find them in department stores or bed and bath stores.

*Beryl Cotter, Red Bluff, CA*

## Bag Bottom Material

Recycle flexible plastic cutting boards for the bottoms of handmade bags. Cover the plastic with a layer of batting for padding and a fabric sleeve, then slip it into the bag.

*Ruth Morehart, Bemidji, MN*

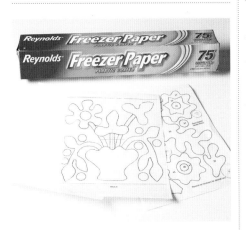

## Quilt Journal

Make a quilt journal using a three-ring binder and page protectors. Use your computer to create a decorative cover page to insert in the front of the binder. Put photos, templates, fabric swatches, and the story of each quilt in the page protectors.

*Donna Buckingham, Leawood, KS*

## Freezer Paper Templates

Use an inkjet printer to print appliqué templates on freezer paper. Scan the appliqué patterns, then cut freezer paper into 8½" × 11" sheets, and print the patterns on them. You will need to hand feed the freezer paper sheets into your printer.

*Beth Pauley, Chesapeake City, MD*

## My Memory Quilt

I use fabrics from each quilt I finish and give away to make a heart block from a favorite paper piecing pattern. I currently have 8 blocks made and am saving them until I get a few more to make a quilt for myself.

*Wendy Maynard,*
*Painesville, OH*

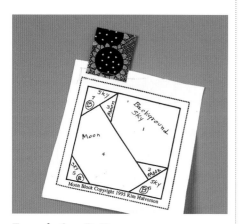

## Foundation Pattern

When I do paper foundation piecing, I worry that I will accidentally use my original pattern. To prevent this, I sew a fabric scrap to the edge of the original so it is easily recognized.

*Florence Hallahan,*
*West Roxbury, MA*

## Traveling Pin Keeper

To keep track of needles and pins when I want to take my hand quilting along with me, I simply put them on a flat magnet and place the magnet in a resealable bag. My needles and pins stay in one place, stuck to the magnet.

When I do projects or classes with children, I give each a colorful magnet to use for their pins and needles.

*Diane Drager, Danube, MN*

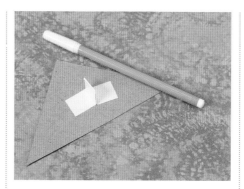

## Template Tab

If you have problems holding your template while drawing around it, use tape to make a handle. (I used white electrician's tape.) If you need to turn the template over to make a reverse shape, the tape handle will flatten out.

*Olga Lehr, David City, NE*

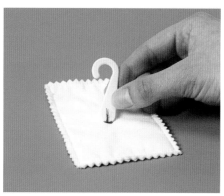

## Project Hanger

The small plastic hooks often attached to a new pair of socks can be used to hang small projects. Lightly whipstitch them to the back of a wallhanging. Use several for larger projects.

*Pat deNeui, Elkader, IA*

## Portable Design Wall

If you don't have room for a design wall, make a portable one from a dressmaker's cardboard cutting board covered with flannel or cotton batting. When you are done for the day, you can fold the board up and store it in a closet or under a bed.

*Diane Tomlinson, Reinbeck, IA*

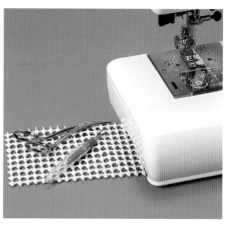

## No-skid Sewing Machine

If your sewing machine has a tendency to "walk away" while you are sewing, put a piece of rug padding under it. Cut a piece the width of your machine plus 6"–8". The extra will keep scissors, seam ripper, bobbins, and other tools close at hand.

*Cecile Myers, Coventry, RI*

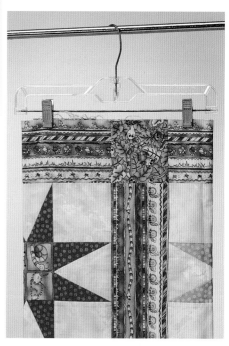

## No Wrinkles

After finishing a quilt top, I iron it and hang it on a pants hanger. This way, it doesn't get wrinkled while it is waiting to be quilted.

*Doris DeGenova,*
*Littleton, CO*

### Take-Along Project Bag

The bags that pillowcases and pillow shams come in make great project bags. They are see-through, zip shut, and are just the right size to toss in your purse so you can take a project along to work on while waiting in a doctor's office or at a child's ball game.

*Susan Messer, Mulliken, MI*

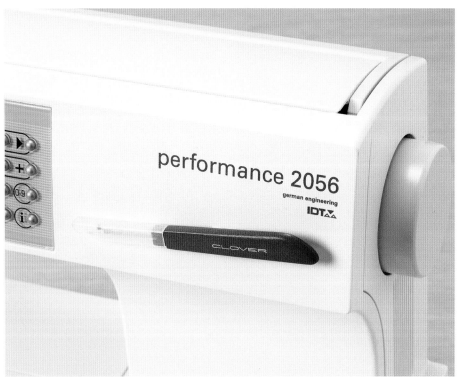

### Handy Tool Holder

I put a small piece of self-adhesive hook-and-loop tape on my seam ripper and the opposite piece on my sewing machine. My seam ripper is always close at hand and easy to find. I also made a small, rectangular pincushion and attached it the same way.

*Roz Agulnik, St. Luc, Quebec*

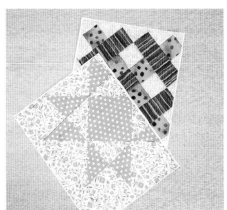

### Fabric Shopping Aid

I make color copies of quilt blocks I am working on to take with me to the fabric store in case I see a fat quarter or fabric that I think will match my colors. This keeps me from buying something that won't match.

*Geraldine Wiktor, Canton, MI*

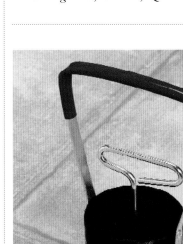

### Magnetic Pick-Up Tool

My friend John McEldowney is very supportive of his wife's quilting passion. He gave her a magnetic tool to pick up pins from the floor. Sweep across the floor to pick up pins; squeeze the handle to release them. This tool costs just a few dollars at a hardware store.

*Pam Ashbaugh for John and Charlotte McEldowney, Tucson, AZ*

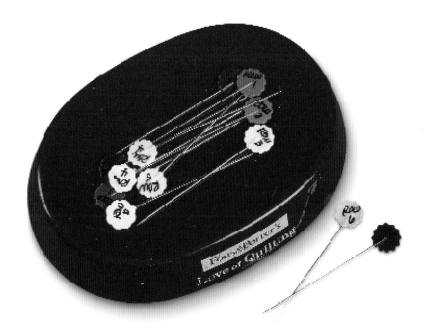

### Tidy Bobbins

I had a problem with thread unwinding from the bobbins in my bobbin case. I bought ⁷⁄₁₆"-diameter clear plastic tubing from a hardware store and cut it into small rings. I cut through one side of a ring and clip it around the bobbin. The thread stays neat and tidy, and I can easily see the thread color.

*Jan Grummer, Ventura, IA*

### No-Fray Appliqué

After basting an appliqué block, I smooth a sheet of Glad® Press 'n Seal™ over it, leaving the area I am working on exposed. The plastic wrap holds the pieces in place and keeps them from fraying until I am ready to stitch the next area. Move over, freezer paper, your cousin has joined the party!

*Jerry Lambert, Warr Acres, OK*

### Scratch Protector

Cover your sewing machine table with Glad® Press'n Seal™ to protect it from pin, needle, and scissor scratches. The plastic wrap contains no adhesives, so it will not damage the surface of the table. It will peel off easily, leaving no residue.

*Patty Goodsell, Arivaca, AZ*

### Pin Labels

Use a fine-tip permanent marker to write row numbers or block positions on flower-head pins. Place pins in quilt blocks to identify where they will be placed in your quilt.

*Rita Lerch, Rising Sun, MD*

### Removing Chalk and Pencil Lines

I use a lightly moistened Mr. Clean® Magic Eraser to remove chalk and pencil lines from fabric.

*Carolyn Reger, Geneva, OH*

### Coffee Cup Bows

At a recent retreat, we had several quilters present, all drinking coffee and tea. To mark our cups, I suggested we each tie a small piece of fabric from the project we were working on to the handle of our cup. This kept them from getting mixed up. It was a hit!

*Mona Pape, Dyersville, IA*

## Quilt Label

I use a unique method to make labels. I program all the label information into my sewing machine. Before adding the binding to a quilt, I stitch the writing on the back half of the binding strip with a strip of tear-away stabilizer underneath. After the binding is sewn on, the writing appears on the back edge.

*Patty Arndt, Austin, TX*

## Handy Gadget Tote

Here's a cute way to keep your gadgets handy when you're on the go. Place six sealable snack bags on a potholder so the bottoms meet in the center. Sew a piece of grosgrain ribbon down the center of potholder, stitching through bags. Fold the potholder and sew a big button on the outside for a closure.

*Susan Hutter, Fort Myers, FL*

## Machine Quilting

I cut the tips off the thumb and forefinger of both of my machine quilting gloves. As I'm quilting, I can pick off stray threads or rethread the needle without taking off my gloves.

*Mary-Jeanine Ibarguen,*
*Altamonte Springs, FL*

## Library Index

I made a list of all my quilting books and tucked it into the glove box of my car. When I'm out shopping, I always have an index of my books, so I don't buy one I already own!

*Nancy Bellis, Kansas City, MO*

## Handy Containers

I use sugar-free drink mix containers for many things in my sewing room. A few examples are: storing my rotary cutter (especially for traveling), storing glue sticks and permanent markers so they don't dry out, and holding a spool of serger thread to use for basting. Punch a hole in the lid and feed the thread through.

*Anne Lawver, Sterling, VA*

## Roll-up Block Mat

To keep my cats from playing with pieces for blocks as I lay them out, I made a roll-up mat like one used for puzzle pieces. I can unroll it, plan my block layout, and roll it back up for safe keeping until I can work on it again. To make your own, glue a rectangle of felt to a cardboard tube from paper towels or wrapping paper. Attach ribbons for ties.

*Kathy Campell, Omaha, NE*

## Tool Organizer

I use a small turntable next to my sewing machine to hold small items such as a seam ripper, scissors, bobbins, pencils, and other sewing gadgets. It keeps my tools contained and easily accessible.

*Joan Reichart, Palm Coast, FL*

## Attaching Buttons

I recently completed a quilt with dozens of buttons—each block had about six. Rather than placing one button at a time, I placed them wrong side up inside a shoe box and sprayed them with temporary adhesive. I could position all the buttons for a block at one time and have them stay in place while I sewed them on by machine using my button foot.

*Connie Baranyk, Binghamton, NY*

## Bag Handles

After making many quilted bags, I have discovered how to make the perfect handle. I wrap a strip of fabric around non-roll elastic and topstitch it down both sides and in the center.

*Audrey Lord, Venus, TX*

## Cleaning Irons

To quickly and inexpensively clean an iron's surface, pour a line of table salt approximately ½" × 6" on a terry towel. Iron back and forth with hot iron. Residue comes right off.

*Norma Cotton, Kalkaska, MI*

## Scrap Quilts

I like to cut my leftover fabrics into usable pieces for scrap quilts. I make a color copy of a quilt I plan to make, write on a sticky note the sizes of the pieces I need to cut, and slip the pattern into a plastic sleeve. The pattern is next to my cutting table, and a plastic storage container labeled with the name of the quilt is ready for the pieces.

*Betsy J. Mott, Shickshinny, PA*

### Storage Boxes

Scrapbooking stores and hobby shops have great boxes of different kinds and sizes that work well for quilting projects and blocks. Staying neat and organized can also be fun!

*Susan Guzinski, Cairo, NE*

### Scoring Foundations

My old tracing wheel comes in handy for scoring the lines on paper foundations. Having them scored makes removing the paper quicker and easier.

*Ruth Haynes, Fairbanks, AK*

### Quilt Label

The day I start working on a quilt, I make binding and a label. I place both in a see-through sealable bag and write the start date on the label. When I finish the quilt, I add the finish date to the label. It's nice to have the binding and label ready when the quilt is done.

*Linda McAdam, Kincaid, KS*

### Scrap Quilts

After I choose a pattern for my next scrap quilt, I place a photo of the quilt on the top of a storage box. When working on other projects, I cut the leftover fabric into pieces for the scrap quilt and put them in the box. Before long, I have another quilt cut and ready to be pieced.

*Gail Alter, Fort Gibson, OKD*

### Quilter's Buddy

If Post-It® notes aren't a quilter's best friend, they are certainly on the buddy list! I keep a pad of 2"-square ones on my sewing table to mark projects in my magazines I want to make, keep track of how many pieces are in a zipper bag, and mark my sewing machine bed for a perfect ¼" seam. I leave myself notes on my sewing machine for particular settings or tensions, and make a list of things I need to pick up on my next fabric shopping trip.

*Delma Atwell, Boise, ID*

## Foundation Piecing

Dress pattern paper works well for foundation piecing. It's thinner than other papers, so you must be careful, but the advantage is that it tears away easily when the block is done.

*Frances K. Howard, Pell City, AL*

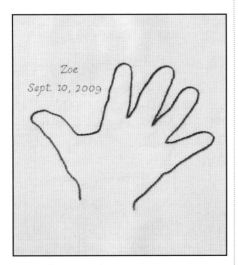

## Growth Record

I trace my grandchildren's handprints on paper, and then onto fabric. I embroider the handprints, and write the child's name and age with a permanent fabric pen. After I've sewn the squares into a quilt top, the kids love to compare their hands with the embroidered handprints to see how they've grown.

*Awdry Aurre, Pontotoc, MS*

## No More Wrinkles

I sometimes find it difficult to iron out the fold crease or the "end" wrinkles in fabric, especially if the fabric has been stored for a while. I discovered that a light spray of a wrinkle release product works wonders to remove the wrinkles and fold line. It also smells good.

*Laura Feldhans,*
*Lake City, IA*

## Fabric Hangers

I wrap selvage edges and narrow strips of fabric around wire clothes hangers, and then use the hangers to hang fabrics in my sewing room closet.

*Cheryl Ellis, White Springs, FL*

## Fabric Counter

When creating a quilt with many fabrics, I cut a small piece from each one and string it on a double thread. When I'm finished with the quilt, I can count the number of fabrics used in the project.

*Carolyn DuPuis, Dousman, WI*

### No-Slip Templates

Use extra fine stick-on sandpaper to make templates that won't slip. Trace template pattern on white paper and rough cut it out (about ¼" outside drawn line). Remove backing from sandpaper and affix paper on the sticky side. Cut out template on drawn line.

*Helen Freeman, Glenpool, OK*

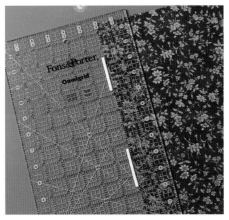

### Simplify Cutting

I use a few strips of correction tape on my ruler to quickly find the line I need when cutting strips of fabric. It removes easily and can be repositioned. The tape can also be used to label blocks or rows.

*Julie Miller, Ankeny, IA*

### Pattern Storage

After I cut out pieces for an appliqué project, I put the pattern, freezer paper pieces, cut fabric pieces, and the selvages with the names of the fabrics into a plastic page protector.

*Devora Olson, Green Valley, AZ*

### Fabric Key Ring

Pin swatches of fabric you need to match on a key ring to take along when you shop. Use a separate safety pin for each project.

*Patricia Miller, West Lancaster, NY*

### Bobbin Keeper

To keep a bobbin with its matching spool of thread, insert a cotton swab through the bobbin and into the top of the spool. Even if they tip over, the bobbin stays in place.

*Linda Bowers, Reynoldsburg, OH*

### Scrappy Binding

I love scrap quilts and hate to waste fabric, so I save my leftover lengths of binding and join them to make binding for scrap quilts. This saves me time later, and the scrappy binding looks great on my quilts.

*Barb Tazelaar, Sioux Center, IA*

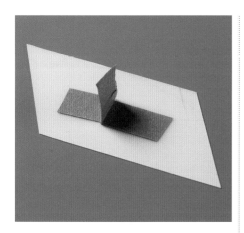

### Template Handle

Sometimes I find it hard to pick up templates, so I cut a piece of painter's tape and make a little "handle." Problem solved!

*Diane Scott, Snowflake, AZ*

### No More Loose Ends

To secure loose ends on spools of thread, wrap them with a piece of elastiband. This is a product made to hold gauze in place, and can be purchased at a medical supply store.

*Vicki Madigan, San Antonio, TX*

### A helpful way to thread needles

To simplify threading needles, cut the thread at an angle so it easily slips through the eye.

*Christianne Drago, Alex, VA*

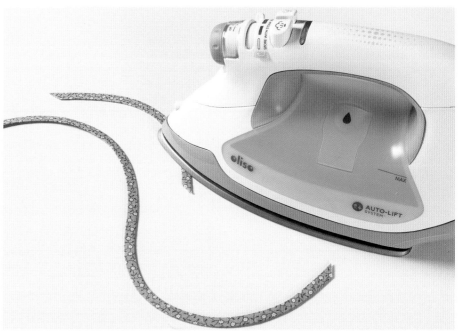

### Appliquéd Bias Strips

For beautifully curved and flat bias strips, steam press in approximate curves before applying. I use metal bias bars to prepare my strips, but this method works with any type of bias.

*Anne Fitts, Vero Beach, FL*

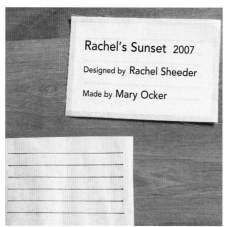

### Quilt Labels

To keep writing on quilt labels neat, draw lines on freezer paper and iron it to the wrong side of the label. Use the lines as guides when you write on the label.

*Georgette Sutton, Biddeford, ME*

### Drawing Lines

When drawing lines on squares to make Triangle-Squares and Flying Geese units, I use an emery board as a straight edge. It won't slip, and keeps the fabric from stretching as you draw.

*Ruby Deputy, Amarillo, TX*

### Cloth Napkins

Use fabrics from your stash to make cloth napkins. Cut a square of fabric and serge or hem the edges. This is a great way to use extra fabric, and, since the napkins are reuseable, they are eco-friendly. Napkins make nice gifts and church bazaar items.

*Mary Crooks, Coralville, IA*

### Homemade Pincushion

I used some leftover fleece to make pincushions. Cut a strip about 2" wide by the width of the fleece. Roll the strip into a tight spiral. Glue the end to the roll. These work great and are cute, too!

*Karen Hartman, Bellevue, OH*

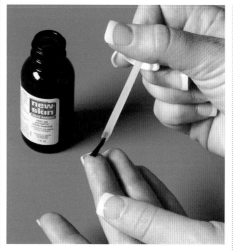

### Fusible Appliqué

Instead of tracing patterns for appliqué, copy the pattern on freezer paper. Put the freezer paper in the copier so it will print on the paper side. On an ironing surface, place the freezer paper pattern on top of the fabric and fusible web on the bottom. Press. Remove the paper from the pieces after cutting them out.

*Kay Turner, Springfield, MO*

### Decorative Switch Plate

Dress up your sewing room with a pretty switch plate. Use a clear plastic switch plate made for use with wallpaper and substitute your favorite fabric for the wallpaper. Iron fusible interfacing to the wrong side of fabric to stabilize, then cut it to size.

*MaryLiz Schoenfeld, Saline, MI*

### Sore Fingers

To prevent sore fingers on my left hand when I hand quilt, I use liquid bandage. Two or more coats are needed for proper protection. It can be peeled off and re-applied as needed. It really works!

*Shirley Niesen, Bradenton, FL*

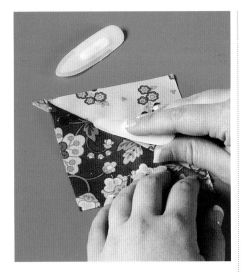

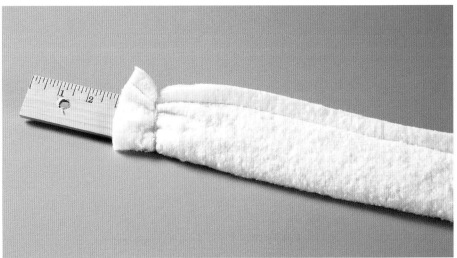

### "Finger" Pressing

I discovered this free gadget at the grocery store. It's the portion of plastic that gets punched out from the handle when plastic milk jugs are formed. Sometimes they're still attached. I use one to press seams, and it works great! If necessary, you can use an emery board to smooth rough edges on the plastic.

*Rea Weigand, Ottawa, KS*

### Leftover Batting

As a machine quilter, I have lots of leftover batting. To make good use of it, I cut a long narrow strip (about 4" × 35"), fold it in half lengthwise, and sew with a narrow seam. Then I slip the batting tube over a yardstick and secure the end with a rubber band. It works great for dusting narrow places such as under the refrigerator and behind furniture.

*Darlene Orschek, North East, PA*

### Labels for Wedding Quilts

I make quilts for wedding gifts, and have found an appropriate way to label them. I scan the wedding invitation, print it on fabric, and attach it to the back of the quilt. It's a special touch that the couple appreciates. I also attach another label that tells who made the quilt, the date it was made, and the occasion.

*Connie Davis, Peculiar, MO*

### Gift Idea

When I give a bundle of fat quarters at our guild's Christmas gift exchange, I include a business card for the shop where I bought it. The recipient of the gift can go back and add to the collection if she needs additional fabric for a project.

*Christine Nichols, Clinton, IA*

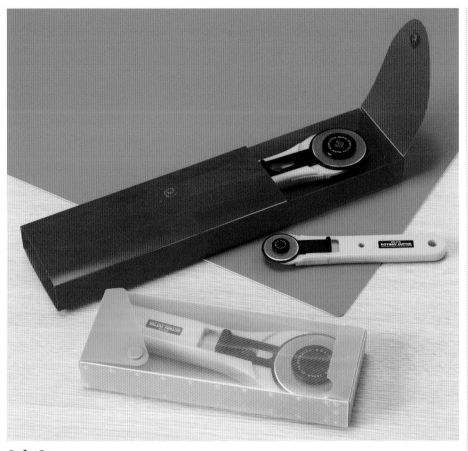

## Safe Storage

Use plastic pencil boxes to store rotary cutters. (These boxes are available at the beginning of each school year and go on sale once school has started.) Even the largest (60 mm) rotary cutter will fit perfectly in the box.

*Ann Rennier, Columbia, MO*

## Quilt Scrapbook

A great way to document your progress as you make a quilt is to take photos at each step and make a scrapbook page.

*Kellie Waterhouse,*
*Spokane Valley, WA*

## Mat Cleaner

Pot scrubbers made from nylon netting work well to remove threads from your rotary cutting mat.

*Lavonne Hook, Hawarden, IA*

## Package Instructions

I save package instructions for rulers, markers, and tools in a plastic storage box so I can easily locate them.

*Carolyn Kolb, Escondido, CA*

## Pressing Fat Quarters

Wash fat quarters and partially dry in the dryer. Place damp fat quarter on a flat surface such as a table or counter-top and smooth fabric with your hands until flat. Add more fat quarters atop first one, smoothing each. Press immediately or take a break, leaving the damp fabrics in a stack. Pressing goes faster since each piece was previously "hand-pressed."

*Vicki Jones, Toledo, OH*

## Picture This!

Instead of using a reducing glass or door peephole glass to view my quilt when laying out the blocks, I use my digital camera. When I look at a photograph, I can easily see if a block needs to be moved or turned. A digital camera is also handy when you've gotten your quilt blocks all laid out and ready to sew, but don't have room to leave them out until you sew them together. Take a digital picture so when you are ready to sew you don't have to redo the layout.

*Bonnie Luedloff, Waconia, MN*

## Thread Organizer

When stitching an embroidery design that uses several colors of thread, use a lipstick tray to organize the spools. Place them in the order they will be used.

*Opal McConnell, Palmyra, NE*

## Portable Needlecase

I hot glued a flat refrigerator magnet, printed side down, to the inside cover of an empty candy mint tin. It makes a handy portable needlecase for on-the-go projects!

*Diane Rose, New Hope, MN*

## Movable Quilt Hanger

My husband put backing for the 3M™ Command™ Adhesive hooks on the backs of two small quilt hangers. I use them to display my seasonal wall quilt, and when the season (and my quilt) changes, I move the quilt hangers to hold a quilt of a different width. I have no holes in the walls and can change my quilts as often as I like.

*Anne Schafroth, Homewood, IL*

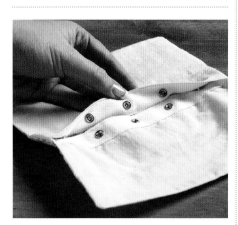

## Pillow Closure

When looking for an easy way to close the back of a pillow, I tried snap tape. It works great!

*Mary White, Tulsa, OK*

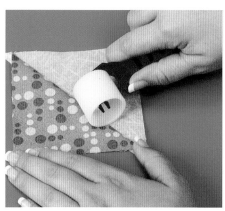

## Handy Seam Roller

When I'm sewing, I quickly "press" seam allowances with a wallpaper seam roller.

*Jean Howes, West Chatham, MA*

## Be Prepared

I make the binding for my quilts as I work on the top. That way, when I complete the quilt, sometimes months or years later, the binding is ready, and I don't have to worry about whether the fabric is still available. I roll my binding and put it in a bag with a label.

*Cindy Burke, McPherson, KS*

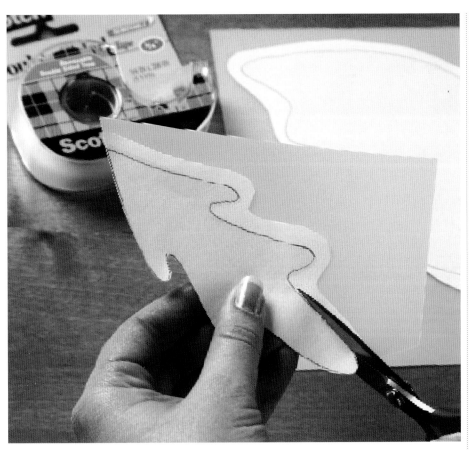

## Saving Buttons

I save buttons from worn-out clothing to use on future projects. I group matching buttons on a bread tie and twist the ends together for quick and easy storage.

*Catherine Griesmer, Rothschild, WI*

## Accurate Templates

To make accurate templates, trace the pattern and roughly cut it out, leaving a little space around the outer line. Use double-stick tape to adhere pattern to template plastic; cut out on cutting line. The template is easier to cut out and more accurate this way.

*Jennifer Stevens, Lincoln, NE*

## Quilt Label

I consider myself to be a "cross crafter" because I enjoy both cross stitch and quilting. To combine my two hobbies, I make cross-stitched labels for my quilts. Sometimes, I stitch a personal note on the label.

*Mary J. Curtis, Maquoketa, IA*

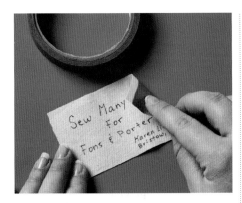

## Easy Writing

Place a strip or two of blue painter's tape on the back of fabric you want to write on. The tape keeps the fabric stable as you write.

*Karen Littlefield, Bristow, VA*

## Mint Tins

I store used rotary cutter blades in purse-size mint tins. When the container is full, I can safely dispose of the blades and tin.

*Brenda Beckstrom, Provo, UT*

## Needle Disposal

When I empty a box of sewing machine needles, I mark an X on each side with a black marking pen. I store my used needles in the box until it is full and then throw the whole thing away safely.

*Sue Cahal, Worthington, KY*

### Mini Iron Storage

I store my craft iron in a one-quart mason jar. It is much more secure than the small stand that came with the iron.

*Becky Beekman, Shadyside, OH*

### Address Labels

I found a good use for extra address labels. I fold them down over the tops of my favorite catalog and magazine pages I want to go back to. This saves time when I'm ready to order from the catalog or look for a quilt that I want to make.

*Eleanor Droege, Rockville, MD*

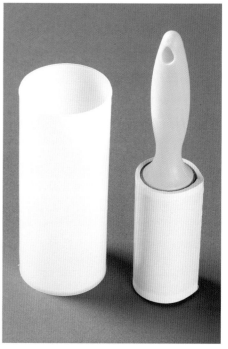

### Secure Thimble

If you have trouble keeping a thimble on your finger, apply a small piece of double-sided tape on the inside. If you prefer, put the tape on your finger before putting the thimble on. It works perfectly and leaves no sticky residue.

*Dorothy Jessen, Pulaski, IA*

### Prevent Rust

Place a silica pack from a medication bottle or a shoe box in with your needles and pins to keep them dry and free from rust.

*Cathy Knowles, Manly, IA*

### Lint Roller Holder

An empty plastic iced tea mix container makes the perfect holder for a lint roller. It's the right diameter and the perfect height for easy access—and you're recycling!

*Pat McDaniel, Indio, CA*

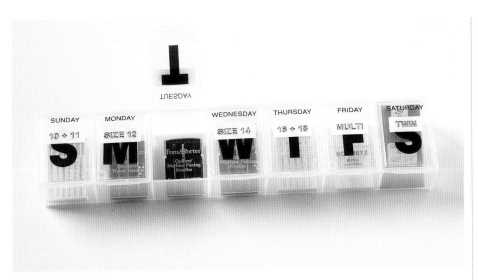

## Needle Storage

A large pillbox is perfect for storing sewing machine needles. I make a label for each section, indicating the size of the needles inside.

*Linda L. Michaelson, Idaho Falls, ID*

## Tool Holder

I use a toothbrush holder for two or three pair of scissors, pencils, pens, and my stiletto. I keep it next to my machine within easy reach. It also holds the long screwdriver that I use when I change throat plates for quilting.

*Donna Daniel, Wichita, KS*

## Saving Selvages

Instead of wasting the selvage edges when I trim my fabric, I save them and make hot pads and rag rugs. I crochet a circle or an oval using a size J or K crochet hook and a single crochet stitch. It's easy, and the results are both pretty and useful.

*Joanne Ganaden, Eleele, HI*

## Practice Quilting

When I find a quilting pattern I like, I put a copy of it in a plastic page protector. I use a dry erase marker to practice the pattern. The lines can be removed with a scrap of batting, and I can practice over and over until I feel comfortable stitching the design.

*Ginny Miller, Boise, ID*

## Keeping a Record

Sometimes my quilt tops are packed away for awhile before I send them off to the machine quilter. When I finish a top, I measure it and take a picture of it. I print the picture and include the measurements so I won't have to measure again. I also include my name, address, and phone number, and make a copy for the machine quilter so she also has this information.

*Tami Johnson, Gothenburg, NE*

# Techniques

The Sew Easy Lessons on pages 44–59 include instructions and step-by-step photos for techniques that will help you accurately piece your next quilt. Each lesson references a quilt pattern on pages 66–127 that uses the technique shown.

# Row Alignment

Follow these easy instructions for perfect alignment when joining pieced rows to unpieced strips as in *Liz's Pinwheel Strippy* quilt on page 76.

1. Fold 1 unpieced strip in quarters and make a mark in seam allowance at each fold. Repeat for 1 pieced row.
2. Join strip to right edge of pieced row, matching marks *(Photo A)*. Repeat for remaining pieced rows.
3. On wrong side, align ruler with seam lines of pinwheel; mark edge of strip *(Photo B)*. Repeat to mark strip across from each pinwheel in each pieced row.
4. Join units, matching marks on strips with points of pinwheels *(Photo C)*.
5. Add remaining strip to left edge of quilt.

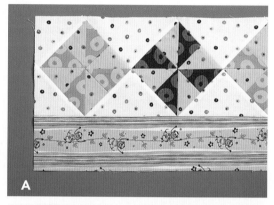

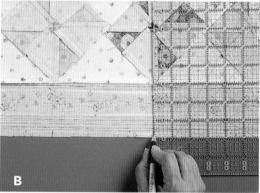

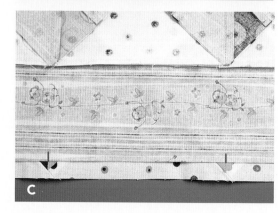

# Sew Easy™

# Trapunto Method for Machine Quilting

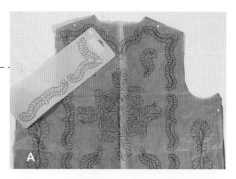

Trapunto (or stuffed quilting) empha-sizes fancy quilting motifs. We love how it looks for feathered quilting designs since it makes the feather areas puff up. This technique is espe-cially dramatic for whole-cloth quilts and shows up best on solid fabrics.

The basic methods for trapunto when machine quilting are the same for a regular home sewing machine as for a longarm quilting machine.

## Special Supplies

Chalk marker, Saral® tracing paper, or other removable marker
Cotton batting
Water-soluble thread
Colored thread that matches top or outer fabric
Blunt-tipped scissors

## Instructions

**1.** Plan placement of quilting motifs (*Photo A*). Use a chalk marker, Saral® transfer paper, or other removable marker to draw quilting designs onto top layer of fabric.

> If you are working on a garment, cut out outer garment pieces with generous seam allowances to allow for drawing up during quilting and trapunto. Leave garment lining pieces as rectangular shapes so they are easier to layer for quilting.
> —Marilyn

**2.** Layer marked top fabric and 2 layers of cotton batting.Using water-soluble thread, stitch design (*Photo B*). Remove from machine.

> This is a great way to use all those scraps of batting left from other projects! —Marilyn

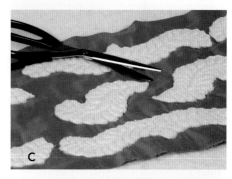

**3.** Using blunt-tipped scissors, trim batting just outside stitching lines of design areas (*Photo C*).
**4.** Layer prepared piece, another layer of cotton batting, and backing fabric. Using thread in color to match top fabric, quilt design (*Photo D*). Stitching will be atop water-soluble thread.
**5.** Add additional background quilting around design motifs to help make tra-punto areas stand out more (*Photo E*).
**6.** Wash piece to remove water-soluble thread.

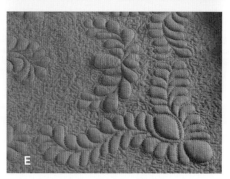

# Paper Foundation Piecing

Paper Foundation piecing is ideal for designs with odd angles and sizes of pieces. Use this method in *Star Rosettes* on page 72 and for the Flower Segments in *Grandmother's Daisy Garden* on page 92.

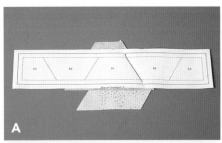

1. Using ruler and pencil, trace all lines and outer edge of foundation pattern onto tracing paper. Number pieces to indicate stitching order.

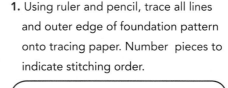

> ## Sew Smart™
> **Save time by making photocopies on special foundation papers. Check photocopied patterns to be sure they are correct size. (Some copiers may distort copy size.) —Liz**

2. Using fabric pieces that are larger than the numbered areas, place fabrics for #1 and #2 right sides together. Position paper pattern atop fabrics with printed side of paper facing you *(Photo A)*. Make sure the fabric for #1 is under that area and that edges of fabrics extend ¼" beyond stitching line between the two sections.

3. Using a short machine stitch so papers will tear off easily later, stitch on line between the two areas, extending stitching into seam allowances at ends of seams.

4. Open out pieces and press or finger press the seam *(Photo B)*. The right sides of the fabric pieces will be facing out on the back side of the paper pattern.

5. Flip the work over and fold back paper pattern on stitched line. Trim seam allowance to ¼", being careful not to cut paper pattern *(Photo C)*.

6. Continue to add pieces in numerical order until pattern is covered. Use rotary cutter and ruler to trim excess paper and fabric along outer pattern lines *(Photo D)*.

7. Carefully tear off foundation paper after blocks are joined.

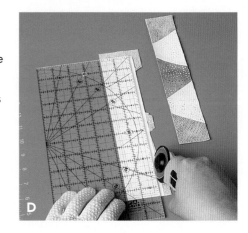

# Paper Foundation Piecing Curves

Use this easy method to make textured, curved leaves for *Grandmother's Daisy Garden* on page 92.

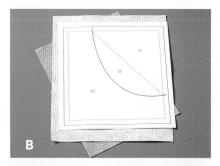

**B**

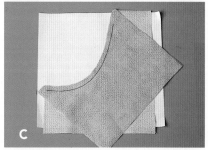

**C**

**1.** Using ruler and pencil, trace all lines and outer edge of foundation pattern onto tracing paper. Number pieces to indicate stitching order.

## Sew **Smart**™
Save time by making photocopies on special foundation papers. Check photocopied patterns to be sure they are correct size. (Some copiers may distort copy size.) —Liz

**2.** Using fabric pieces that are larger than the numbered areas, place fabrics for #1 and #2 right sides together. Position paper pattern atop fabrics with printed side of paper facing you *(Photo A)*. Make sure the fabric for #2 is under that area and extends ¼" beyond curved stitching line between the two sections and that edge of fabric for #1 extends ¼" beyond stitching line between sections #1 and #2.

## Sew **Smart**™
Fabric piece #2 is much larger than you think you'll need. Pleats take up a lot of room. Make sure the extra fabric for #2 is in the "cup" of the curve. —Marianne

**3.** Using a short machine stitch so papers will tear off easily later, stitch on the curved line between the two areas, extending stitching into seam allowances at ends of seams *(Photo B)*. Trim seam allowance to ¼" *(Photo C)*.

**4.** Open out pieces and finger press pleats in piece #2 *(Photo D)*. Baste pleats in place.

**5.** Continue to add pieces in numerical order until pattern is covered. Use rotary cutter and ruler to trim excess paper and fabric along outer pattern lines *(Photo E)*.

**6.** Join pieced sections to complete Stem Unit *(Photo F)*.

**7.** Carefully tear off foundation paper after blocks are joined.

**D**

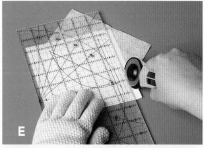

**E**

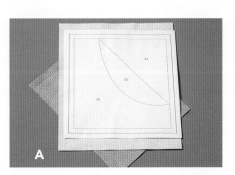

**A**

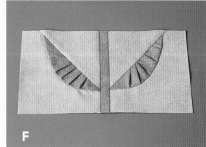

**F**

# Windowing Fusible Appliqué

Try our method for utilizing fusible web that keeps appliqués soft and flexible.
This is a great technique for *Berry Wreath* (page 80) and *Stars* (page 86).

Choose a lightweight "sewable" fusible product. The staff at your favorite quilt shop can recommend brands. Always read and follow manufacturer's instructions for proper fusing time and iron temperature.

**B**

> ## Sew Smart™
> **Fused shapes will be the reverse of the pattern you trace. If it's important for an object to face a certain direction, make a reverse pattern to trace. We do this quickly by tracing the design on tracing paper, then turning the paper over and tracing the design through onto the other side of the paper.**
> **—Marianne**

Follow manufacturer's instructions to fuse web side of each shape to wrong side of appliqué fabric.

4. Cut out appliqués, cutting carefully on drawn outline *(Photo D)*. Only a thin band of fusible web frames the shape.

5. Peel off paper backing *(Photo E)*. Position appliqué in place on background fabric, and follow manufacturer's instructions to fuse shapes in place.

> ## Sew Smart™
> **If you have trouble peeling off the paper backing, try scoring paper with a pin to give you an edge to begin with. —Liz**

**C**

1. Trace appliqué motifs onto paper side of fusible web, making a separate tracing for each appliqué needed *(Photo A)*.

2. Roughly cut out drawn appliqué shapes, cutting about ¼" outside drawn lines *(Photo B)*.

3. "Window" the fusible by trimming out the interior of the shape, leaving a scant ¼" inside drawn line *(Photo C)*.

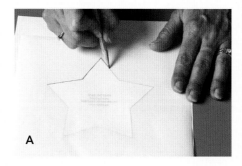

**A**

**D**

**E**

# Piecing Quarter-Square Triangle Borders

The key to perfect borders made with quarter-square triangles is proper alignment. Don't lose points—follow these instructions to learn this method for making the borders for the *Berry Wreath* quilt on page 80.

1. On wrong side of each triangle, mark dots at intersections of seamlines *(Photo A)*.

2. Place 2 triangles together, right sides facing. Stick a pin straight through each dot on top triangle, coming out through dots on bottom triangle *(Photo B)*.

   **NOTE:** Corners will not be aligned. It's only important to align dots for these triangles.

3. Pin triangles together, remove vertical pins *(Photo C)*. Sew seam.

4. Press seam allowance toward one side; trim points as shown *(Photo D)*.

5. Add remaining triangles in the same manner *(Photo E)*.

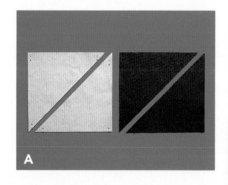

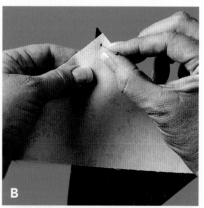

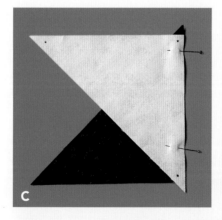

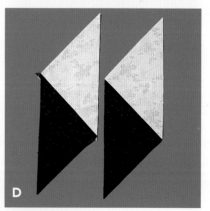

# Sew Easy™

# Mitering Corners

Follow these instructions to make perfect mitered inner borders for *Berry Wreath* on page 80 corners or for *Stars* on page 86.

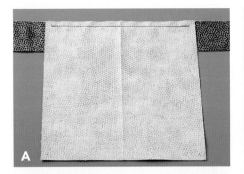

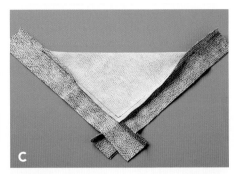

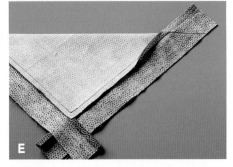

1. Fold block in half and place a pin at the center of block side. Fold border strip in half and mark center with pin.

2. With right sides facing and raw edges aligned, match center pins on block and border strip. The strip will extend beyond block edges. Do not trim the strip.

3. Sew border strip to block. Start and stop stitching ¼" from corner of block, backstitching at each end *(Photo A)*.

4. Press seam allowance toward border strip. Add remaining border strips in the same manner *(Photo B)*.

5. With right sides facing, fold block diagonally, aligning raw edges of adjacent sides *(Photo C)*.

6. Open seam allowance; align a ruler along the diagonal fold. Mark a line from seam to raw edge *(Photo D)*.

7. Stitch on line, backstitching at beginning, and stitching out to raw edge *(Photo E)*.

8. Unfold block and make sure strips lie flat. Correct stitching if necessary. Trim seam allowance to ¼".

9. Miter remaining corners. Press corner seams open *(Photo F)*.

# Piped Binding

Narrow piping inserted along the edge of your binding can be the perfect finish.
Best of all, you can make and finish this binding completely by sewing machine.
Try this technique for *Stars* on page 86.

A

B

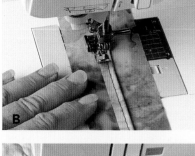

C

D

## Supplies

Fabric to make 2¼"-wide binding strips

Fabric to make ¾"-wide continuous
    fabric strip to cover cording

$\frac{1}{16}$"-diameter cording

Zipper foot or cording foot for
sewing machine

Clear monofilament nylon thread

Glue Stick

## Instructions

1. Begin by measuring around the perimeter of your quilt; add 20" to this measurement to allow for mitering corners of binding and finishing the ends. From binding fabric, make 2¼"-wide straight-grain binding this length. From piping cover fabric, make ¾"-wide straight-grain strip this length.

2. Fold piping strip in half, enclosing cording. Baste close to cording using zipper or cording foot (*Photo A*).

3. To mark the center of the binding strip, fold it in half, wrong sides facing, and press. Open binding back out so it is flat; press lightly if desired.

4. Using zipper or cording foot, stitch piping to center fold line of binding (*Photo B*). Fold binding in half with wrong sides facing.

5. Trim excess batting and quilt back so ditch between piping and binding will align with first binding stitching when binding is sewn to quilt.

6. Working from the quilt back, align raw edge of binding with raw edge of quilt back. Piping fabric will be on top of binding fabric. Stitch binding to quilt (*Photo C*). Miter corners and join the ends just as when applying regular binding.

7. Bring binding over edge of quilt to front. Use clear monofilament thread (or thread that matches the piping cover fabric) and a zipper or cording foot to topstitch through all layers in the ditch between the piping and the binding (*Photo D*).

# Quick Hourglass Units

Try our quick and easy method to make Hourglass Units without cutting triangles. The Fons & Porter Quarter Inch Seam Marker helps you draw stitching lines quickly. *Lucy's Dinner Plate* on page 98 uses this technique.

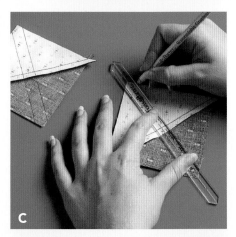

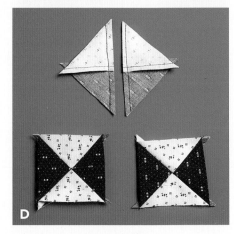

1. From 1 light and 1 dark fabric, cut 1 square 1¼" larger than the desired finished size of the Hourglass Unit. For example, to make an Hourglass Unit that will finish 2⅝" for *Lucy's Dinner Plate*, cut 3⅞" squares.

2. On wrong side of light square, place Quarter Inch Seam Marker diagonally across square, with yellow center line positioned exactly at corners. Mark stitching guidelines along both sides of Quarter Inch Seam Marker (*Photo A*).

**NOTE:** If you are not using the Fons & Porter Quarter Inch Seam Marker, draw a diagonal line from corner to corner across square. Then draw sewing lines on each side of the first line, ¼" away.

3. Place light square atop dark square, right sides facing; stitch along marked sewing lines.

4. Cut between rows of stitching to make two triangle-squares (*Photo B*). Press seams toward darker fabric.

5. On wrong side of one triangle-square, place Quarter Inch Seam Marker diagonally across square, perpendicular to seam, aligning yellow center line with corners of square. Mark stitching guidelines along both sides of Quarter Inch Seam Marker (*Photo C*). See note in #2 if you are not using the Fons & Porter Quarter Inch Seam Marker.

6. Place triangle-square with drawn line atop matching triangle-square, right sides facing and opposite fabrics facing. Stitch along both drawn lines. Cut between rows of stitching to create 2 Hourglass Units (*Photo D*). Press seam allowances to 1 side.

# Cutting 60° Diamonds and Pyramids

Use the Fons & Porter 60° Diamonds Ruler and 60° Pyramids Ruler to make easy work of cutting pieces for *Blue Lagoon* on page 104.

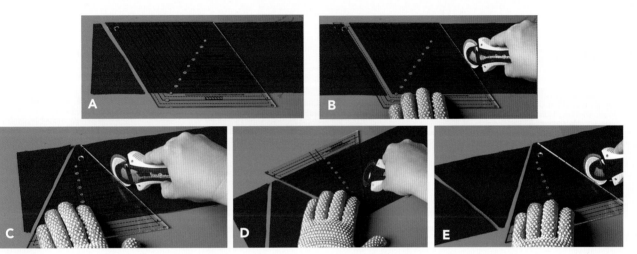

## Diamonds

**1.** To cut diamonds, cut strip desired width (for *Blue Lagoon*, cut strips 5½" wide).

**2.** Referring to strip width numbers along lower section of Fons & Porter 60° Diamonds ruler, find the solid black line on the ruler that corresponds to the width of strip you cut.

**3.** Beginning at left end of fabric strip, place ruler so bottom solid line for desired size diamond is aligned with bottom edge of strip, and cut along left side of ruler *(Photo A)*.

> ## Sew **Smart**™
> **To cut the maximum number of pieces from a fabric strip, open out the strip so you will be cutting through a single layer. To cut many pieces, layer several strips and cut them at the same time. —Liz**

**4.** Move ruler to the right; align desired line of ruler with slanted edge and bottom edge of strip. Cut along right slanted edge of ruler to cut diamond *(Photo B)*.

**5.** Repeat Step #4 to cut required number of diamonds.

## Pyramids

**1.** To cut pyramids, cut strip desired width (for *Blue Lagoon*, cut strips 5½" wide).

**2.** Referring to strip width numbers along lower section of Fons & Porter 60° Pyramids ruler, find the solid black line on the ruler that corresponds to the width of strip you cut.

**3.** Beginning at left end of fabric strip, place ruler atop strip so solid line on ruler is along bottom edge of fabric strip. Trim along left slanted edge of ruler.

> ## Sew **Smart**™
> **If you cut left handed, work from the right end of the fabric strip and begin by cutting along the right edge of the ruler. —Marianne**

**4.** Cut along right slanted edge of ruler to cut one pyramid triangle *(Photo C)*.

**5.** To cut second pyramid triangle, rotate ruler so solid line is on top edge of strip and angled side of ruler is aligned with slanted edge of strip. Cut along slanted edge of ruler *(Photo D)*.

**4.** Continue in this manner to cut required number of Pyramids *(Photo E)*.

# Set-In Seams

Use these tips and techniques for set-in seams as you stitch
*Montana Hearth* on page 109 or *Prairie Stars* on page 66.

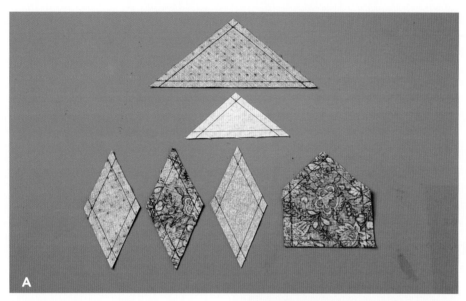

A

**1.** Mark a dot on wrong side of each diamond, A and B triangle, and C piece at intersection of ¼" seam allowances as shown in *Photo A*.

> ## Sew **Smart**™
> We like to draw a stitching line on the wrong side of every piece.
> —Marianne

**2.** Join 1 dark red print diamond and 1 medium red print diamond, stitching from center point to dot; backstitch at dot *(Photo B)*.

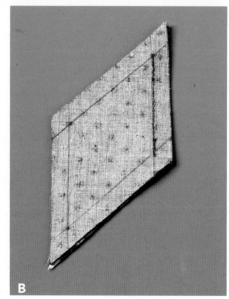

B

**3.** Pin A triangle to diamond unit, aligning outer points. Stitch from dot to dot; backstitch *(Photo C)*.

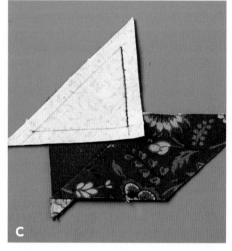

C

**4.** Stitch triangle to adjoining diamond unit to complete 1 side unit *(Photo D)*. Make 4 side units.

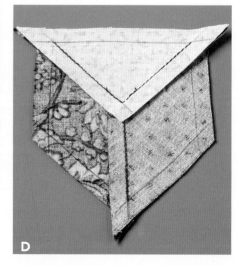

D

**5.** Join side units *(Photo E)*.

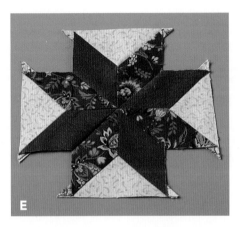

### Sew Smart™

Except for the outer edge of block, always stitch from dot to dot. This will keep seam allowances free to allow you to set in pieces. —Liz

**6.** In the same manner, set in A triangles to complete star unit *(Photo F)*.

**7.** Referring to *Block Assembly Diagram*, continue in this manner, joining 2 gold print diamonds, 1 C piece, and 2 A triangles to make each outer side unit. Make 4 outer side units. Join 1 C and 2 A triangles to make each outer corner unit. Make 4 outer corner units.

Block Assembly Diagram

**8.** Add outer corner units and outer side units to star unit, setting in seams *(Photo G)*.

**9.** Add dark red print B triangles to outer corner units to complete block *(Block Diagram)*.

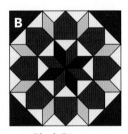

Block Diagram

# Quick Triangle-Squares

Use this quick method to make the triangle-squares for *Pick-Up Sticks* on page 112. The Fons & Porter Quarter Inch Seam Marker offers a neat way to mark accurate sewing lines for this method.

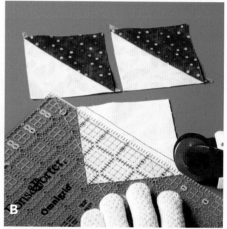

1. From each of 2 fabrics, cut 1 square ⅞" larger than the desired finished size of the triangle-square. For example, to make a triangle-square that will finish 2¼", as in the *Pick-Up Sticks* quilt on page 112, cut 3⅛" squares.

2. On wrong side of lighter square, place the Quarter Inch Seam Marker diagonally across the square, with the yellow center line positioned exactly at opposite corners. Mark stitching lines along both sides of the Quarter Inch Seam Marker *(Photo A)*.

3. Place light square atop darker square, right sides facing; stitch along both marked sewing lines.

4. Cut between rows of stitching to make 2 triangle-squares *(Photo B)*.

**NOTE:** If not using the Fons & Porter Quarter Inch Seam Marker, cut 3⅛" brown and light tan print squares in half diagonally to make half-square triangles. Join 1 brown print triangle and 1 light print triangle to make a triangle-square.

# Sewing Curved Seams

When you're making a Drunkard's Path or any quilt with curved pieces, use these tips to make sewing curved seams easier. *Graphix* (page 116) includes curved seams.

**1.** After cutting the background "crust" and the quarter-circle "pie" pieces, mark the center of the curve on each piece by folding in half and creasing or making a small clip *(Photo A)*.

**2.** Working with the background "crust" on top, pin pieces together at curve centers, taking a small bite. At the end of the seam, align pieces and pin, taking a large bite *(Photo B)*.

**3.** Align pieces at beginning of seam. Stitch to the middle of the curve. Use your fingertips to keep curved edges aligned or control the top fabric and keep edges aligned with a wooden skewer *(Photo C)*.

**4.** Leaving the needle in the fabric, raise the presser foot. "Fluff" the top "crust" fabric back toward where you have sewn *(Photo D)*.

**5.** Align curved edges for the second half of the seam and stitch to about 1" from end of seam. Stop again and "fluff" the top fabric so ending edges are also aligned. Sew to the end of the seam *(Photo E)*.

**6.** Gently press seam allowance toward background "crust" piece.

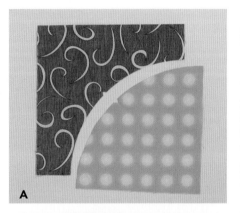

A

C

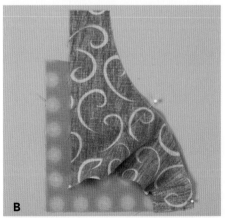

B

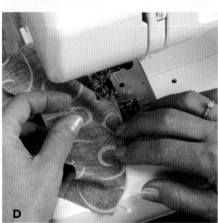

D

E

# Sew Easy™
# Strip Sets

A strip set is a group of strips that have been sewn together lengthwise in a particular sequence. Completed strip sets are later cut into smaller segments to use as blocks or as portions of blocks. Follow these instructions to make Liz's *Double Nine Patch* on page 120.

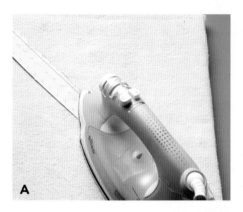

**A**

1. Perfectly straight and accurately cut strips are essential for strip sets. If strips are cut across folded width of fabric, open strips to see that they are straight. If strips are not cut exactly perpendicular to fold, they will bow where they were folded, making a crooked strip.

2. To make a strip set, pair two strips with right sides facing and raw edges aligned. Machine stitch with ¼" seam. Press seam to one side. Begin by pressing strips flat, just as you have sewn them, to set stitching (*Photo A*). Fold top fabric strip back, revealing right side of seam and strip set. Gently, with side of iron, press seam open on right side with seam allowances to one side (*Photo B*). Strip set should be straight, without any distortion along outside edges.

3. Add third strip to complete strip set. If making strip sets with more than three strips, join strips in pairs and then sew pairs together. Make required number of strip sets.

### Sew Smart™
Pinning strip edges in a few places will help prevent bottom strip in pair from drawing up. Alternating sewing direction from strip to strip will help keep strip sets straight.
—Liz

### Sew Smart™
Measure the height of your strip set. For example, strip set for **Liz's Double Nine Patch** should measure exactly 3½".
If it is not 3½", adjust seams to get the correct measurement.
—Marianne

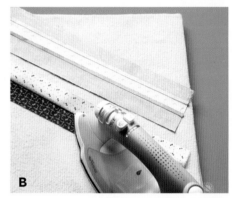

**B**

4. Aligning horizontal lines on ruler with long edge and seam lines of strip set, trim uneven end of strip set.

5. Keeping horizontal lines on ruler aligned with strip set, cut required width segments (*Photo C*). Segments for *Double Nine Patch* are cut 1½" wide. Cut required number of strip set segments.

**C**

### Sew Smart™
To cut multiple segments at once, stack up to three strip sets, right sides up, offsetting seam allowances (*Photo D*). —Liz

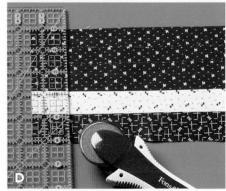

**D**

# Sew Easy™
# Mirror Images

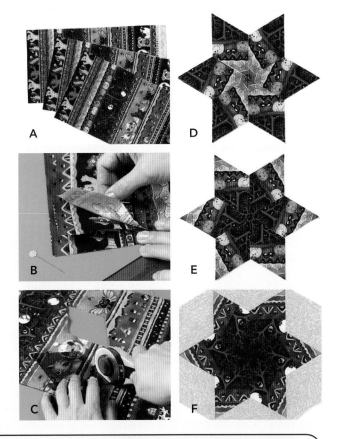

If you are cutting many stars from the same fabric, try this speedy technique to cut sets of six identical diamonds.
Large-scale fabrics or novelty prints work well for this method.
*Lumniosity Stars* (page 124) uses this technique.

1. Focusing on a specific motif in your fabric to find the repeat, cut 6 sections of fabric which are exactly alike *(Photo A)*.
2. Stack the 6 layers so that the motifs are perfectly lined up. Push a flatheaded pin through each layer in exactly the same spot to align layers *(Photo B)*. Pin layers in several places to keep them from slipping when cutting.
3. Position template on fabric pieces and cut through all layers *(Photo C)*. Repeat to cut required number of pieces for project.
4. Lay out 1 group of 6 diamonds to make a star *(Photo D)*. The same group of pieces make a totally different star when the diamonds are turned in the opposite direction *(Photo E)*.
5. Join diamonds and add setting pieces to complete 1 Hexagon Star Block *(Photo F)*.

## Sew Smart™

**Design mirrors which are attached at one side can be moved around the fabric to find an area that will make an interesting block.**

BY **Marilyn Badger**.

# Quilting the Quilt
## Practice Makes Perfect

Build your custom quilting skills by learning new designs.

Longarm quilters are faced with many different styles of quilts on which to perform our magic. Choosing the best quilting design, thread, and batting is often left to our discretion. We must know which designs work best on certain quilt tops and also recognize our own limitations when it comes to quilting those designs.

In today's longarm quilting world, the trend is to quilt free-motion designs rather than overall pantograph-type patterns. This requires me to have a virtual encyclopedia of free-motion designs in my memory bank.

When developing a new design, I make sure I can draw it evenly in a continuous line to fill an 8" × 10" sheet of paper. Only then do I feel confident that I can step up to the machine and stitch out the design. I also stitch the design on a muslin quilt sandwich to archive in a sample book I keep for future reference.

Since 2002, I have been working on projects with Claudia Clark Myers of Duluth, Minnesota. We collaborate to create several quilts each year for competition. Claudia has a wonderful color sense and is exceptionally talented at creating and piecing difficult quilts.

*Great Balls of Fire quilt designed and made by Claudia Clark Myers; machine quilted by Marilyn Badger.*

**Detail:** Knowing what the designer was thinking while creating this quilt helped me create just the right quilting designs.

Since these are her original designs, I do my utmost to generate original and exciting quilting for each one. It doesn't just happen—I spend a lot of time developing what I think are the perfect motifs. Over time, I have learned some tricks that help in the process.

Claudia often relates to me her inspiration for designing the quilt. I find great value in that information for my design work. One example is our *Great Balls of Fire* quilt (shown at left), a variation of the Mariner's Compass pattern. We created it to enter in the Theme Category of the 2005 Machine Quilters Showcase, All That Jazz!

Claudia designed the quilt with large open spaces for my quilting. I wanted to carry the circle theme into those open spaces and create feathers around them. First, I used my circle attachment to create circles ¾" away from the compass units. Then, using chalk, I made marks in one-inch increments around the circles. The marks provided guidelines so I could quilt free-motion feathers that were uniform rather than simply random. I could also stitch evenly inside the circle. I accented the feathers with scrolls and flames which tie in with the title of the quilt. I enhanced the feather quilting by stippling the remaining background. Claudia added beads and crystals after I completed the quilting.

I'm happy to report *Great Balls of Fire* won first place at Machine Quilters Showcase. It was also awarded first place Traditional Quilt at Pacific International Quilt Festival.

# TRY THESE FREE-MOTION DESIGNS

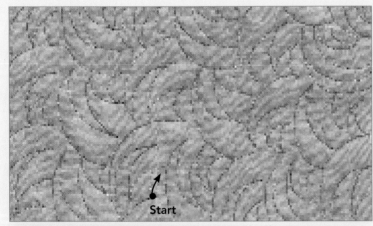

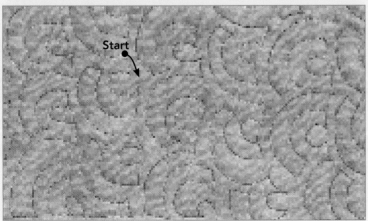

**Arcs** A repeated arc is a great design to start with if you are just learning free-motion quilting. Practice it on paper; then stitch it. When you feel you can stitch a motif right side up, upside down, and sideways, you have mastered the design. I call this design 1-2-3 because you stitch an arc at least 3 times. Graduate the arcs from small to larger, always echo quilting the first shape. The secret is to make the first arc small so the last one doesn't get too large. If you stitch the echos an odd number of times, such as 3 (or 5 as in my sample), you will be moving in one direction. Stitch an even number of echos to change direction.

**Fans** When you have mastered the arc design, try changing it by squaring off the ends to make little fans. This looks like a very simple design, but it is a bit difficult to master. Follow my designs with your finger to see how they work. Practice turning corners and working the design every direction. Draw it on paper; then quilt.

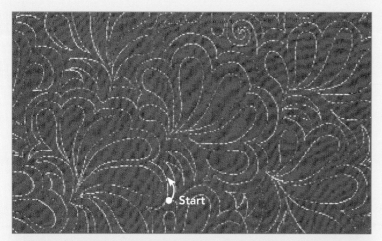

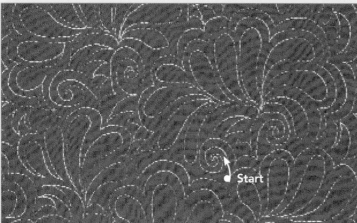

**Plumes** Next, use arcs as a base for feather plumes. There are three basic steps to this design.

1. Make 3 or 4 arcs;

2. Work a feather around the final arc; and

3. Echo the feather all the way around.

Each time, make arcs, then feather, then echo. The side on which you end your arc will determine the direction of your feather. You'll need to know how to quilt feathers right side up, upside down, and sideways.

**Plumes with Curlicues** The next design is the same as the one above, but has curlicues thrown in on each side. Start with a curlicue aiming left, then echo, do a small arc, and another curlicue aimed right. Echo back to the middle and fill in the space between with arcs. Keep going until you have a large enough arc to work the free-motion feather around, then echo, and you're ready to start another curlicue.

## TIPS SUCCESSFUL FREE-MOTION QUILTING

**Whether quilting with a longarm or domestic sewing machine:**

- Practice drawing designs on paper before you start to stitch.
- Remain calm. The more relaxed you are, the more proficient you will become. Remember to breathe.
- Don't get in a hurry. Quilting too fast will cause you to round out your points and sacrifice accuracy. This advice applies even if you have a stitch regulated machine.
- Use a metronome to help you quilt at a steady and rhythmic speed. I like to listen to music with a regular beat.

## AUTHOR

Marilyn Badger has been producing award-winning quilts since 1991. She received the award for Best Longarm Quilt at the AQS Quilt Show & Contest at Paducah in 2004. She has been a guest on over 50 PBS quilting shows with Fons & Porter and Kaye Wood, as well as Quilt Central and Simply Quilts. Marilyn has taught longarm classes in the United States, Canada, Australia, and Japan. When not quilting, Marilyn loves to play golf. ✵

BY **Dawn Cavanaugh**. National Director of Education, American Professional Quilting Systems

# Quilting the Quilt

## Patchwork Borders

While many quilters choose to frame their patchwork with plain fabric borders, others use patchwork to make the border itself stand out. Pieced borders present unique challenges for machine quilting, whether you stand at a longarm or sit at your sewing machine to quilt.

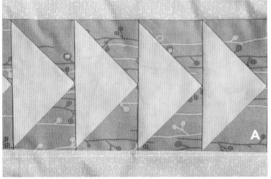

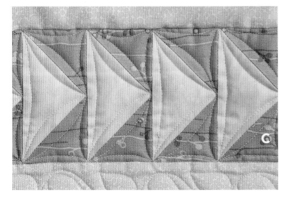

### Making Pieced Borders

If you choose a patchwork border for your quilt, remember that precise piecing is of utmost importance. If your seam allowances are not accurate, or your pressing is a bit lazy, your border will not fit correctly. While you can ease a pieced border to fit your quilt top just as you would a plain fabric border, discrepancies will be much more noticeable.

Plan your patchwork border so that bias edges of patches are not along the outer edge of the border. Backstitch the seams that will be on the quilt's outer edge. These seams can easily pull apart when a longarm quilter attaches your quilt to the frame, distorting the edge of the quilt and causing undue rippling. Stabilize the outer edge of the border by stay stitching $1/8$" from the outer edge. Use a stitch length 2.5–3.0mm, and stitch a straight line along the edge, taking care not to stretch the patchwork or flip the seam allowances in the wrong direction.

### Quilting Pieced Borders

Quilting designs for your pieced border can be simple or dramatic, but it is important to keep the amount of quilting consistent with the amount of quilting in the quilt center. Too little quilting along the border will cause it to ripple, while too much will distort the center. Strive for balance between the two.

Stitching in the ditch between the border and the quilt center will stabilize the border and keep it straight and true. *Photo A* shows a Flying Geese border before quilting. It appears to be straight. In *Photo B*, the large triangle and background triangles were quilted with continuous curve quilting lines, but the "ditch" above and below the pieced section was not stitched. Notice that the border now seems wobbly, even though it started out straight. In *Photo C*, the ditch above and below the border was stitched, giving crisp visual separation to the border while maintaining its straight appearance.

I think stitching in the ditch stabilizes a quilt and gives it the appearance that everything is square. Quilt judges also like to see stabilizing stitches to maintain straight seam lines. However, stitching in the ditch can be boring if it is the only quilting element used. In the design examples here, look for areas where I combined stitching in the ditch with other quilting shapes, and areas where I left the ditches unstitched. Use these as a guide to determine if your quilt needs that extra effort to stay straight, or if it will be fine without it.

I have included a few quilting designs for two popular pieced border styles—Flying Geese and Checkerboard—to get you started. You'll also find diagrams to illustrate the stitching path I used to reduce or eliminate starts and stops.

Since I am a longarm quilter, I work left to right when I draw a border design because I quilt along the border length as it is loaded on my frame. If you sit down to quilt, simply turn the diagrams vertically to simulate how you would quilt them on a domestic sewing machine.

Many of the designs I have included for you actually include two or more stitching paths, even though some could be completed in one pass. Using two stitching lines allows me to sew from left to right, reducing tension problems and thread breakage. Sometimes it is worth adding an extra start and stop along the way if it means that my stitches will look nicer on both the front and the back of the quilt.

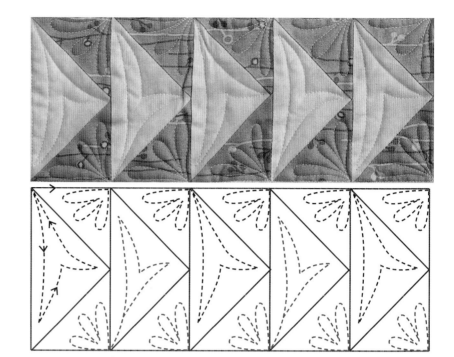

First Pass—"Downward" design is stitched in every other goose, teardrops are stitched in every background triangle (stitch in the ditch to get from one to another).

Second Pass—Ditch is used to travel from one design to the next; teardrops are stitched in every triangle; "upward" design all remaining geese.

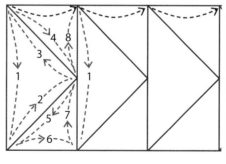 

First Pass—Stitch continuous curves across top.

Second Pass—Follow steps 1–8; repeat.

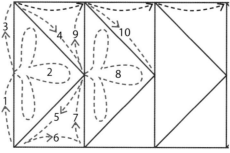 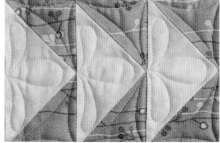

First Pass—Stitch continuous curves across top.

Second Pass—Follow steps 1–9; stitch design inside goose triangle along the way.

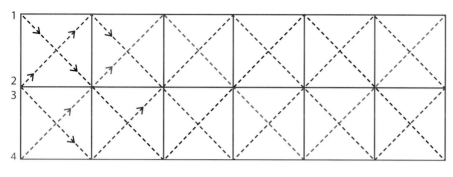

Pass 1 --------- Pass 2 ---------- Pass 3 ---------- Pass 4 ----------

Stitch straight lines, using corners of patchwork as a guide.

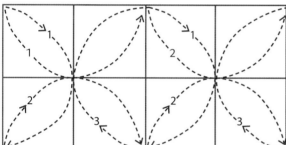

First Pass—Repeat steps 1–3.

Second Pass—Stitch curved lines across top squares.

First Pass—Stitch continuous curves across top.

Second Pass—Repeat steps 1–7 across.

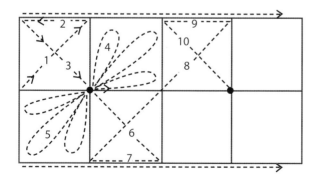
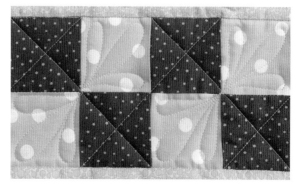

First Pass —Backstitch short distances in the ditch *(step 2)* to complete "X." Then, add the top and bottom teardrops when you reach the intersection (red dot). Continue Steps 6–10 to add "X," adding teardrops at each red dot.

Second Pass—Stitch in the ditch along top and bottom (you will be stitching over previous stitching in some areas).

QUILT BY **Liz Porter and Shon McMain.**
MACHINE QUILTED BY **Jean Nolte**.

# Prairie Stars

Traditionally, the small diamonds for a Prairie Star quilt were individually cut and joined. Quick cutting and piecing methods make short work of assembling the stars for this stunning quilt. Trapunto in the large background squares and rectangles emphasizes the beautiful machine quilting.

**PROJECT RATING: CHALLENGING**

**Size:** 91" × 109"
**Blocks:** 20 (18") Prairie Stars

## MATERIALS

7½ yards cream print for
background, borders, and binding
¼ yard each of 36 assorted prints
for pieced stars and
border stars
6 (6") squares assorted prints for
border stars
¾ yard brown print for vine
8¼ yards backing fabric
King-size quilt batting
Paper-backed fusible web (optional)
Tracing paper
Colored pencils or crayons

## Cutting

Measurements include ¼" seam allowances. Follow manufacturer's instructions for using fusible web. Border star pattern is on page 71.

**From cream print, cut:**

- 1 (2⅝-yard) piece. From this, cut 4 (10"-wide) **lengthwise** strips for borders.
- 4 (11"-wide) strips. From strips, cut 12 (11") C squares.
- 2 (8¾"-wide) strips. From strips, cut 5 (8¾") squares. Cut squares in half diagonally in both directions to make 20 quarter-square B triangles (2 are extra).
- 11 (5¾"-wide) strips. From strips, cut 14 (5¾" × 11") D rectangles and 35 (5¾") A squares.
- 11 (2¼"-wide) strips for binding.

**From each ¼-yard piece, cut:**

- 1 Border Star.
- 5 (1¾"-wide) strips for pieced stars. (Strips need to be at least 24" long for piecing stars.)

**From each 6" square, cut:**

- 1 Border Star

**From brown print, cut:**

- 430" of 1½"-wide bias strips. Fold bias in thirds and press to prepare vine for appliqué.

## Star Assembly

**1.** Trace *Coloring Diagram* onto tracing paper. Determine fabric placement for pieced star and color diagram using colored pencils or crayons. Refer to *Sample Colored Star Diagram* for an example.

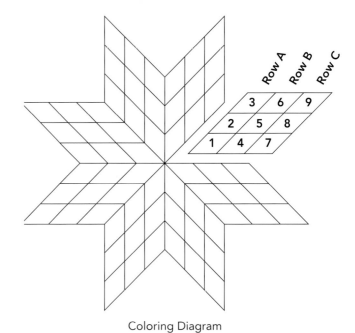

Coloring Diagram

Sample Colored Star Diagram

**2.** Join strips for diamonds #1–#3 into a strip set, offsetting strips by approximately 1¾" as shown in *Row A Diagram*. Trim left end of strip set at a 45-degree angle. Place 1¾" mark on ruler atop angled cut. Cut along edge of ruler to make a segment of joined diamonds that is 1¾" wide. Cut 8 Row A segments.

**3.** In the same manner, join strips #4–#6 and #7–#9 into strip sets and cut 8 segments from each strip set for Row B and Row C (*Row B Diagram* and *Row C Diagram*).

**4.** Referring to *Star Point Assembly Diagrams,* lay out 1 each of Row A, B, and C. Join rows to complete 1 star point. Make 8 star points.

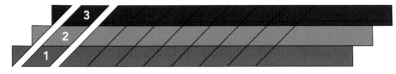

Row A Diagram

Row B Diagram

Row C Diagram

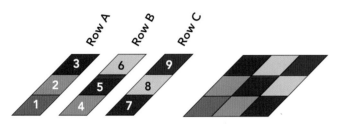

Star Point Assembly Diagrams

**5.** Lay out 8 star points as shown in *Star Assembly Diagram*. Join to make 1 Prairie Star *(Prairie Star Diagram)*. Make 20 Prairie Stars.

Star Assembly Diagram

Prairie Star Diagram

## Quilt Assembly

**1.** Lay out Prairie Stars as shown in photo on page 71.

**2.** Join 4 Prairie Stars by setting in 1 B triangle at each end of row and 3 A squares between stars as shown in *Star Row Diagram* on page 70. Make 5 star rows. Refer to *Sew Easy: Set-In Seams* on page 54.

Star Row Diagram

Row Joining Diagram

**3.** Join rows by setting in 1 D rectangle at each end of row and 3 C squares and 4 A squares between stars as shown in *Row Joining Diagram*.

**4.** Set in D rectangles, A squares, and B triangles around perimeter of quilt to complete quilt center.

## Border Assembly

**1.** Measure quilt length. Cut 2 border strips this length. Add borders to quilt sides. Measure quilt width, including side borders. Cut 2 border strips this length. Add borders to top and bottom edges of quilt.

**2.** Referring to photo on page 71, position vine and stars atop quilt border. Refer to *Sew Easy: Windowing Fusible Appliqué* on page 48 on to quilt top borders. Blanket stitch around stars (*Blanket Stitch Diagram*).

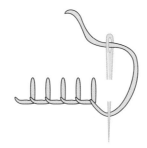

Blanket Stitch Diagram

## Quilting and Finishing

**1.** Divide backing into 3 (2¾-yard) lengths. Join panels lengthwise. Seams will run horizontally.

**2.** Mark desired quilting designs in background C and D pieces. We used a feathered square design for C squares and half the design for D rectangles. Refer to *Quilting the Quilt: Fine Feathers* on page 141.

**3.** If you plan to add trapunto to quilting motifs, refer to *Sew Easy: Trapunto Method for Machine Quilting* on page 45 to baste batting beneath quilting design areas.

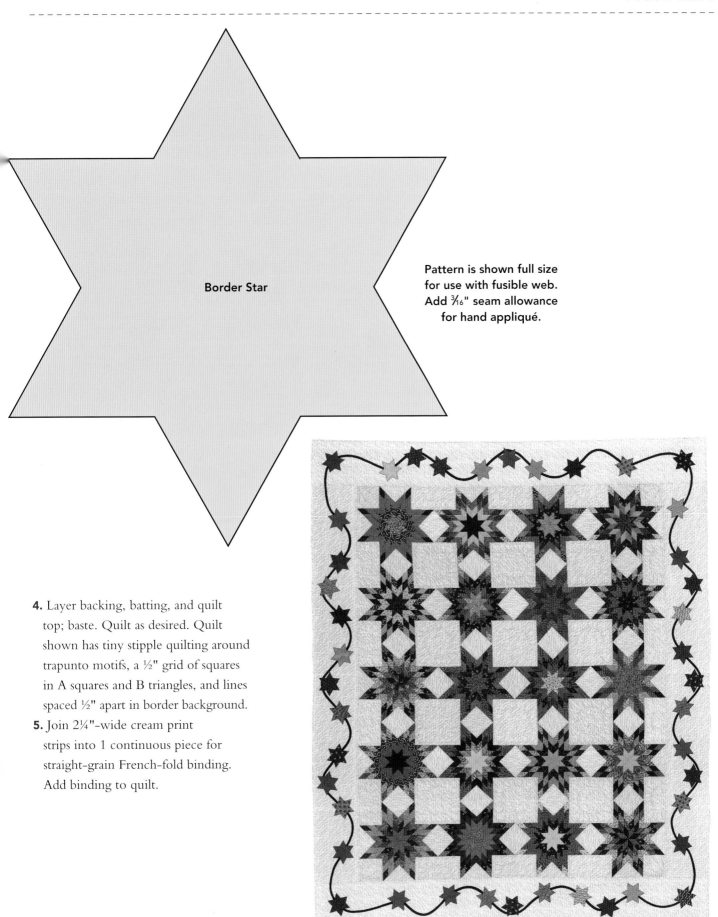

**Border Star**

Pattern is shown full size
for use with fusible web.
Add ³⁄₁₆" seam allowance
for hand appliqué.

**4.** Layer backing, batting, and quilt
top; baste. Quilt as desired. Quilt
shown has tiny stipple quilting around
trapunto motifs, a ½" grid of squares
in A squares and B triangles, and lines
spaced ½" apart in border background.

**5.** Join 2¼"-wide cream print
strips into 1 continuous piece for
straight-grain French-fold binding.
Add binding to quilt.

# Star Rosettes

Nancy Mahoney used red and black prints to provide perfect contrast with the white print background in her quilt. The blocks are easily pieced on paper foundations.

PROJECT RATING: INTERMEDIATE
**Size:** 58" × 70"
**Blocks:** 20 (12") Star blocks

## MATERIALS

1⅜ yards red print

1 yard red stripe

1 yard red check

¾ yard black print for blocks

1¾ yards black floral for border and binding

1⅜ yards red-on-white print

3⅛ yards black-on-white print

Paper for foundations

3½ yards backing fabric

Twin-size quilt batting

## Cutting

Measurements include ¼" seam allowances. Border strips are exact length needed. You may want to make them longer to allow for piecing variations. Foundation patterns are on page 75. For instructions on paper foundation piecing, see *Sew Easy: Paper Foundation Piecing* on page 46.

**From red print, cut:**

- 8 (5½"-wide) strips. From strips, cut 80 (5½" × 4") A1 rectangles.

**From red stripe, cut:**

- 10 (3"-wide) strips. From strips, cut 80 (3" × 5") B1 rectangles.

**From red check, cut:**

- 7 (4½"-wide) strips. From strips, cut 80 (4½" × 3") B4 rectangles.

**From black print, cut:**

- 8 (3"-wide) strips. From strips, cut 80 (3" × 4") A4 rectangles.

**From black floral, cut:**

- 4 (5½"-wide) **lengthwise** strips. From strips, cut 2 (5½" × 60½") side borders and 2 (5½" × 58½") top and bottom borders.
- 5 (2¼"-wide) **lengthwise** strips for binding.

**From red-on-white print, cut:**

- 15 (3"-wide) strips. From strips, cut a total of 240 (3" × 2½") rectangles (A5, B2, B3).

**From black-on-white print, cut:**

- 10 (6"-wide) strips. From strips, cut a total of 160 (6" × 2½") rectangles (A2, A3).
- 13 (3½"-wide) strips. From strips, cut a total of 160 (3½" × 3") rectangles (B5, B6).

## Block Assembly

1. Trace or photocopy 80 each of Foundation A and B.
2. Referring to *Foundation Diagrams*, paper piece foundations in numerical order. Make 80 Foundation A and 80 Foundation B.

**A**          **B**

Foundation Diagrams

3. Lay out 4 Foundation A and 4 Foundation B as shown in *Block Assembly Diagrams* on page 74. Join to complete 1 block *(Block Diagram)*. Make 20 blocks.

## Quilt Assembly

1. Lay out blocks as shown in *Quilt Top Assembly Diagram* on page 74. Join into rows; join rows to complete quilt center.
2. Add side borders to quilt center. Add top and bottom borders to quilt.

**Block Assembly Diagrams**

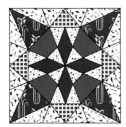

**Block Diagram**

## Finishing

**1.** Divide backing into 2 (1¾-yard) lengths. Join panels lengthwise. Seam will run horizontally.

**2.** Layer backing, batting, and quilt top; baste. Quilt as desired. Quilt shown was quilted with a leaf design in the blocks, and with overlapping hearts in the border *(Quilting Diagram)*.

**3.** Join 2¼"-wide black floral strips into 1 continuous piece for straight-grain French-fold binding. Add binding to quilt.

**Quilting Diagram**

**Quilt Top Assembly Diagram**

 **WEB** EXTRA

To download size options and *Quilt Top Assembly Diagrams* for this project visit our Web site at www.FonsandPorter.com/starrosesizes.

## DESIGNER

A prolific quiltmaker and author of twelve books, Nancy Mahoney is also a teacher and fabric designer. She enjoys making traditional quilts using new techniques that make quiltmaking easy and fun. ✳

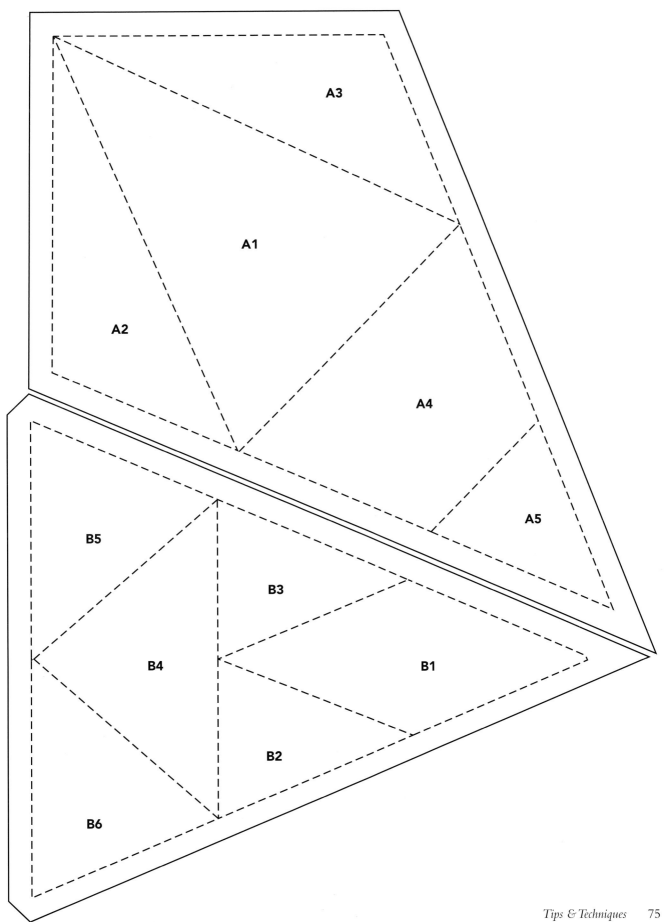

QUILT BY **Liz Porter.**

HAND QUILTED BY **Deena Yoder.**

# Pinwheel Strippy

Liz says, "I love scrappy quilts and strippy sets! I made the Pinwheel blocks from my stash, so there are dozens of different prints in this quilt."

**PROJECT RATING: INTERMEDIATE**

**Size:** 72" × 91"

**Blocks:** 120 (4") Pinwheel blocks

## MATERIALS

- 20 fat eighths★ assorted dark prints in black, red, green, brown, purple, blue, and pink
- 20 fat eighths★ light shirting prints for blocks
- 2¾ yards cheddar print for background
- 3¼ yards navy print for strips, border, and binding
- Fons & Porter Half & Quarter Ruler (optional)
- 5½ yards backing fabric
- Full-size quilt batting
- ★fat eighth = 9" × 20"

## Cutting

Measurements include ¼" seam allowances. Instructions are written for using the Fons & Porter Half & Quarter Ruler. If not using this ruler, follow cutting **NOTES**. Border strips are exact length needed. You may want to make them longer to allow for piecing variations.

> ### Sew **Smart**™
> Layer 1 dark print strip and 1 light shirting print strip, right sides facing. From strips, cut pairs of half-square A triangles. Do not separate triangles. —Liz

**From dark print fat eighths, cut a total of:**

- 60 (2½"-wide) strips. From strips, cut 120 sets of 4 matching A triangles.
  **NOTE**: If not using the Fons & Porter Half & Quarter Ruler, cut a total of 60 (2⅞"-wide) strips. From strips, cut 120 sets of 2 matching (2⅞") squares. Cut squares in half diagonally to make 480 half-square A triangles.

**From light shirting print fat eighths, cut a total of:**

- 60 (2½"-wide) strips. From strips, cut 120 sets of 4 matching A triangles.
  **NOTE**: If not using the Fons & Porter Half & Quarter Ruler, cut a total of 60 (2⅞"-wide) strips. From strips, cut 120 sets of 2 matching (2⅞") squares. Cut squares in half diagonally to make 480 half-square A triangles.

**From cheddar print, cut:**

- 12 (6⅞"-wide) strips. From strips, cut 56 (6⅞") squares. Cut squares in half diagonally in both directions to make 224 quarter-square B triangles.
- 2 (3¾"-wide) strips. From strips, cut 16 (3¾") squares. Cut squares in half diagonally to make 32 half-square C triangles.

**From navy print, cut:**

- 9 (2¼"-wide) strips for binding.
- 11 (3½"-wide) **lengthwise** strips. From strips, cut 9 (3½" × 85⅜") strips and 2 (3½" × 72¾") top and bottom borders.

## Pinwheel Block Assembly

**1.** Join 1 dark print A triangle and 1 light print A triangle as shown in *Triangle-Square Diagrams*. Make 4 matching triangle-squares.

Triangle-Square Diagrams

**2.** Lay out triangle-squares as shown in *Pinwheel Block Assembly Diagram*. Join into rows; join rows to complete 1 Pinwheel block *(Pinwheel Block Diagram)*. Make 120 Pinwheel blocks.

Pinwheel Block Assembly Diagram

Pinwheel Block Diagram

## Row Assembly

**1.** Referring to *Quilt Top Assembly Diagram*, lay out 15 blocks, 28 cheddar print B triangles, and 4 cheddar print C triangles as shown. Join into diagonal rows; join rows to complete 1 pieced row.

**2.** Make 8 pieced rows.

## Quilt Assembly

**1.** Lay out pieced rows and navy print strips as shown in *Quilt Top Assembly Diagram*. Join to complete quilt center.

### Sew **Smart**™
Refer to *Sew Easy: Row Alignment* on page 44 for perfect alignment of pieced rows and navy print strips. —Liz

**2.** Add navy print top and bottom borders to quilt.

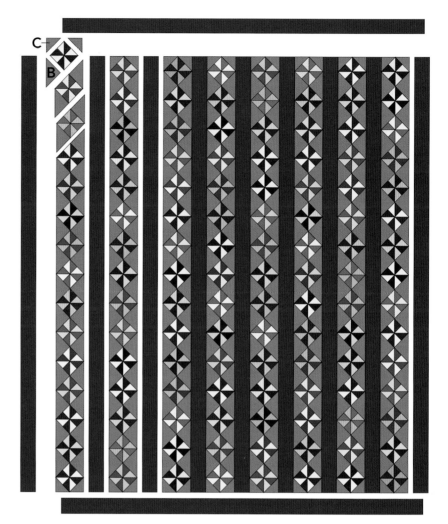

Quilt Top Assembly Diagram

## Finishing

**1.** Divide backing into 2 (2¾-yard) lengths. Cut 1 piece in half lengthwise to make 2 narrow panels. Join 1 narrow panel to each side of wider panel; press seam allowances toward narrow panels.

**2.** Layer backing, batting, and quilt top; baste. Quilt as desired. Quilt shown was outline quilted in blocks and with a football-shaped design in navy strips and borders *(Quilting Diagram)*.

**3.** Join 2¼"-wide navy print strips into 1 continuous piece for straight-grain French-fold binding. Add binding to quilt.

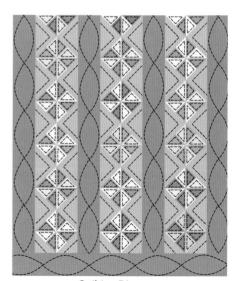

Quilting Diagram

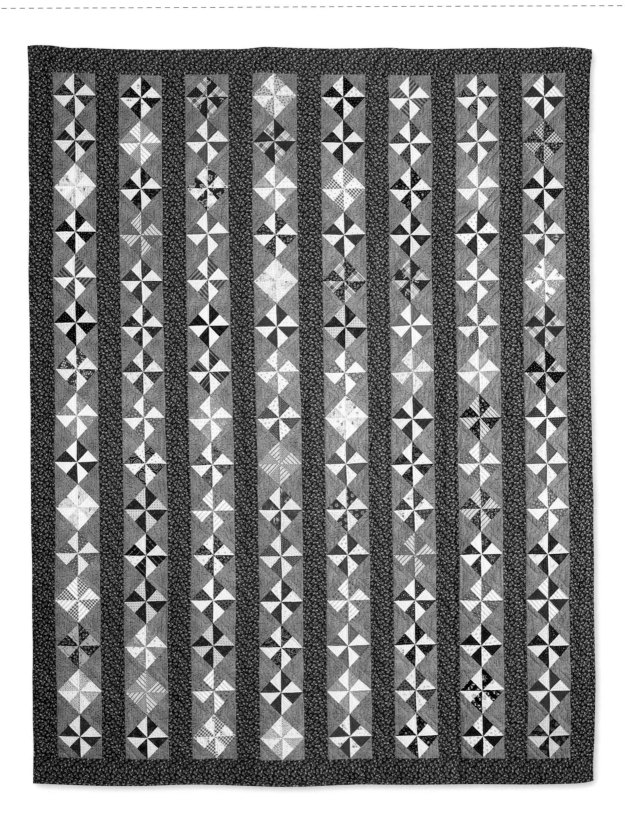

# Berry Wreath

Nancy Mahoney combined piecing and appliqué for this lovely throw. It's made in Christmasy red and green, but it is beautiful any time of year.

**PROJECT RATING: INTERMEDIATE**
**Size:** 63" × 63"
**Blocks:** 9 (15") blocks

## MATERIALS

⅜ yard tan floral

2½ yards beige print for background

1 yard dark green print for blocks and borders

1⅝ yards medium green print for appliqué and outer border

1¼ yards stripe for border

¾ yard pink print #1 for pieced blocks

¾ yard pink print #2 for berries and binding

Paper-backed fusible web

4 yards backing fabric

Twin-size quilt batting

## Cutting

Measurements include ¼" seam allowances. Outer border strips are exact length needed. You may want to cut them longer to allow for piecing variations. Patterns for appliqué are on pages 84. Follow manufacturer's instructions for using fusible web. .

**From tan floral, cut:**

• 1 (7½"-wide) strip. From strip, cut 5 (7½") A squares.

**From beige print, cut:**

• 2 (15½"-wide) strips. From strips, cut 4 (15½") G squares.

• 2 (7¼"-wide) strips. From strips, cut 8 (7¼") squares. Cut squares in half diagonally in both directions to make 32 quarter-square H triangles.

• 2 (5⅞"-wide) strips. From strips, cut 10 (5⅞") squares. Cut squares in half diagonally to make 20 half-square B triangles.

• 1 (3⅞"-wide) strip. From strip, cut 4 (3⅞") squares. Cut squares in half diagonally to make 8 half-square J triangles.

• 2 (3⅜"-wide) strips. From strips, cut 20 (3⅜") squares. Cut squares in half diagonally to make 40 half-square E triangles.

• 5 (3"-wide) strips. From strips, cut 20 (3" × 5½") C rectangles and 20 (3") D squares.

**From dark green print, cut:**

• 3 (5½"-wide) strips. From strips, cut 16 (5½") F squares.

• 12 (1¼"-wide) strips. Piece strips to make 8 (1¼" × 57") border strips.

**From medium green print, cut:**

• 2 (7¼"-wide) strips. From strips, cut 9 (7¼") squares. Cut squares in half diagonally in both directions to make 36 quarter-square H triangles.

• 1 (3½"-wide) strip. From strip, cut 4 (3½") I squares.

• 7 (2"-wide) strips. Piece strips to make 2 (2" × 63½") top and bottom outer borders and 2 (2" × 60½") side outer borders.

• 4 Circles.

  **NOTE:** If you prefer appliquéd bias strips for the circles, cut 4 (1⅛" × 30") bias strips. Fold strips in thirds; press folds in place to prepare circles for appliqué.

- 32 Leaves.
- 20 Leaves reversed.

**From stripe, cut:**

- 6 (3½"-wide) strips. Piece strips to make 4 (3½" × 57") border strips.

**From pink print #1, cut:**

- 2 (3⅜"-wide) strips. From strips, cut 20 (3⅜") squares. Cut squares in half diagonally to make 40 half-square E triangles.
- 5 (3"-wide) strips. From strips, cut 56 (3") D squares.

**From pink print #2, cut:**

- 7 (2¼"-wide) strips for binding.
- 52 Berries.

## Pieced Block Assembly

**1.** Lay out 1 tan floral A square and 4 beige print B triangles as shown in *Block Center Diagrams.* Join to complete 1 block center. Make 5 block centers.

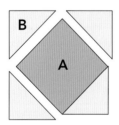

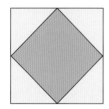

Block Center Diagrams

**2.** Referring to *Flying Geese Unit Diagrams,* place 1 pink print #1 D square atop 1 beige print C rectangle, right sides facing. Stitch diagonally from corner to corner as shown. Trim ¼" beyond stitching. Press open to reveal triangle. Repeat

for opposite end of rectangle to complete 1 Flying Geese Unit. Make 20 Flying Geese Units.

Flying Geese Unit Diagrams

**3.** Join 1 pink print #1 E triangle and 1 beige print E triangle as shown in *Triangle-Square Diagrams.* Make 40 triangle-squares.

Triangle-Square Diagrams

**4.** Lay out block center, 4 Flying Geese Units, 8 triangle-squares, and 4 beige print D squares as shown in *Block Assembly Diagram.* Join into rows; join rows to complete 1 block *(Block Diagram).* Make 5 blocks.

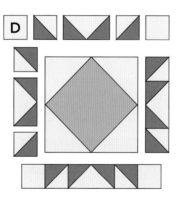

Block Assembly Diagram

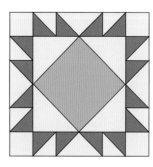

Block Diagram

## Appliqué Block Assembly

**1.** Referring to *Block Background Diagrams,* place 1 dark green print F square atop 1 beige print G square, right sides facing. Stitch diagonally from corner to corner as shown. Trim ¼" beyond stitching. Press open to reveal triangle. Repeat for remaining corners of square.

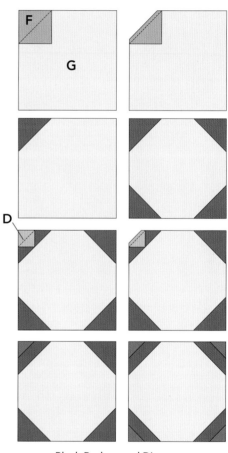

Block Background Diagrams

**2.** In the same manner, place 1 pink print #1 D square atop each corner of block background; stitch diagonally, trim, and press to complete 1 block background.

**3.** Arrange 1 medium green print Circle, 8 Leaves, 5 Leaves reversed, and 13 Berries atop block background as shown in *Appliqué Block Diagram.* Fuse in place; machine appliqué using matching thread. Make 4 appliqué blocks.

Appliqué Block Diagram

## Inner Border Assembly

**1.** Add 1 dark green print border strip to each side of 1 stripe border strip to make 1 inner border.

**2.** Make 4 inner borders

## Outer Border Assembly

**1.** Referring to *Quilt Top Assembly Diagram*, join 9 medium green print H triangles, 8 beige print H triangles, and 2 beige print J triangles to make 1 middle border. See *Sew Easy: Piecing Quarter-Square Triangle Borders* on page 49.

**2.** Make 4 middle borders.

## Quilt Assembly

**1.** Lay out blocks as shown in *Quilt Top Assembly Diagram*. Join into rows; join rows to complete quilt center.

**2.** Add inner borders, mitering corners.

For instructions on mitering corners, go to page 50 *Sew Easy: Mitering Corners.*

**3.** Add 1 middle border to each side of quilt.

**4.** Add 1 medium green print I square to each end of remaining middle borders. Add borders to top and bottom of quilt.

**5.** Add side outer borders to quilt. Add top and bottom outer borders to quilt.

Quilt Top Assembly Diagram

## Finishing

**1.** Divide backing into 2 (2-yard) lengths. Cut 1 piece in half lengthwise to make 2 narrow panels. Join 1 narrow panel to each side of wider panel; press seam allowances toward wider panel.

**2.** Layer backing, batting, and quilt top; baste. Quilt as desired. Quilt shown was quilted in the ditch, with a fleur-de-lis design in center of pieced blocks, loops in striped border, and a scallop and fern design in middle and outer borders *(Quilting Diagram)*.

**3.** Join 2¼"-wide pink print #2 strips into 1 continuous piece for straight-grain French-fold binding. Add binding to quilt.

Quilting Diagram

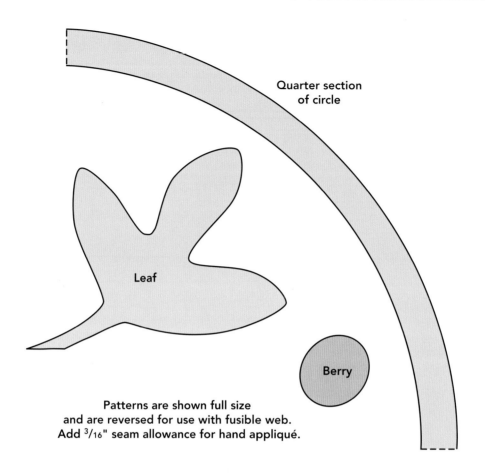

Quarter section
of circle

Leaf

Berry

Patterns are shown full size
and are reversed for use with fusible web.
Add 3/16" seam allowance for hand appliqué.

## DESIGNER

Author, teacher, fabric designer, and award-winning quiltmaker Nancy Mahoney has enjoyed making quilts for more than twenty years. She enjoys combining traditional blocks and updated techniques to create dazzling quilts. She has authored twelve books, all published by Martingale & Company.

## TRIED & TRUE

We gave our block a summery look with prints in the colors of sand and water. Fabrics are batiks by Hoffman.

# Stars

Designer Sarah Vedeler machine appliquéd bright stars on a
sky blue background to make this dazzling quilt.

**PROJECT RATING: INTERMEDIATE**

**Size:** 58" × 58"
**Blocks:** 4 (16") Star blocks
4 (8" × 16") Star blocks
12 (8") Star blocks

## MATERIALS

1⅛ yards blue print for blocks

½ yard dark blue print for binding

1⅜ yards teal print for blocks and
  outer border

⅜ yard green print for blocks

1 yard red print for blocks

½ yard purple print for blocks

1 fat quarter★ each pink and yellow
  prints for stars

1¼ yards orange print for stars,
  inner border, and piping

Paper-backed fusible web

7 yards ¹⁄₁₆"-diameter cording for
  piping

Susan K. Cleveland's Piping Hot
  Binding Tool (optional)

3¾ yards backing fabric

Twin-size quilt batting

★fat quarter = 18" × 20"

## Cutting

Measurements include ¼" seam
allowances. Patterns for appliqué are
on page 91. Follow manufacturer's
instructions for using fusible web.

**From blue print, cut:**

• 2 (12½"-wide) strips. From strips,
  cut 4 (12½") E squares and
  4 (12½" × 4½") J rectangles.

• 2 (6½"-wide) strips. From strips,
  cut 12 (6½") G squares.

**From dark blue print, cut:**

• 7 (2¼"-wide) strips for binding.

**From teal print, cut:**

• 7 (4½"-wide) strips. Piece strips to
  make 4 (4½" × 62") outer borders.

• 8 (1½"-wide) strips. From strips, cut
  32 (1½" × 10") H rectangles.

**From green print, cut:**

• 4 (2½"-wide) strips. From strips,
  cut 8 (2½" × 18") F rectangles.

**From red print, cut:**

• 4 (2½"-wide) strips. From strips,
  cut 8 (2½" × 18") F rectangles.

• 4 (1½"-wide) strips. From strips,
  cut 16 (1½" × 10") H rectangles.

• 2 Large Starbursts.

• 2 Small Starbursts.

**From purple print, cut:**

• 6 (2½"-wide) strips. From strips,
  cut 8 (2½" × 18") F rectangles and
  8 (2½" × 10") I rectangles.

**From pink print fat quarter, cut:**

• 4 Star A.

• 4 Star B.

• 4 Star C.

• 4 Star D.

**From yellow print fat quarter, cut:**

• 2 Star A.

• 2 Star B.

• 8 Star C.

• 4 Star D.

**From orange print, cut:**

• 7 (1½"-wide) strips. Piece strips to
  make 4 (1½" × 62") inner borders.

• 7 (¾"-wide) strips. Piece strips to
  make continuous strip approximately
  245" long.

  **NOTE:** If using the Piping Hot
  Binding Tool, cut strips according to
  instructions with tool.

• 2 Large Starbursts.

• 2 Small Starbursts.

• 6 Star A.

• 6 Star B.

• 4 Star D.

## Block Assembly

1. Position 1 red print Large Starburst and 1 orange print Small Starburst atop 1 blue print E square as shown in *Block 1 Appliqué Diagram*. Fuse in place; machine appliqué using matching thread and blanket stitch.

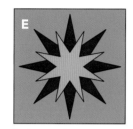

Block 1 Appliqué Diagram

**NOTE:** To reduce bulk in layered appliqué pieces, refer to *Sew Easy: Windowing Fusible Appliqué* on page 48.

2. Add green print F rectangles to sides of appliquéd square, mitering corners, to complete 1 green Block 1 *(Block 1 Diagrams)*. Make 2 green Block 1.

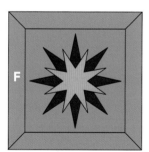

**Make 2**

**Make 2**

Block 1 Diagrams

**NOTE:** For instructions on mitering corners, see *Sew Easy: Mitering Corners* on page 50.

3. In the same manner, make 2 red Block 1 using 1 blue print E square, 1 orange print Large Starburst, 1 red print Small Starburst, and 4 red print F rectangles in each.

4. Position 1 pink print Star A, 1 orange print Star B, and 1 yellow print Star C atop 1 blue print G square as shown in *Block 2 Appliqué Diagram*. Fuse in place, machine appliqué using matching thread and blanket stitch. Add teal print H rectangles, mitering corners, to complete 1 Block 2 *(Block 2 Diagrams)*. Make 4 Block 2.

Block 2 Appliqué Diagram

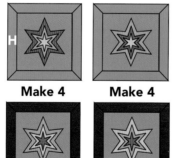

**Make 4**     **Make 4**

**Make 2**     **Make 2**

Block 2 Diagrams

5. In the same manner, make 4 Block 2 using 1 blue print G square, 1 orange print Star A, 1 pink print Star B, and 1 yellow print Star C, and 4 teal print H rectangles. Make 2 Block 2 using 1 blue print G square, 1 orange print

Star A, 1 yellow print Star B, and 1 pink print Star C, and 4 red print H rectangles. Make 2 Block 2 using 1 blue print G square, 1 yellow print Star A, 1 orange print Star B, and 1 pink print Star C, and 4 red print H rectangles.

6. Position 1 yellow print Star D, 1 orange print Star D, and 1 pink print Star D atop 1 blue print J rectangle as shown in *Block 3 Appliqué Diagram*. Fuse in place; machine appliqué using matching thread and blanket stitch. Add purple print F and I rectangles, mitering corners, to complete 1 Block 3 *(Block 3 Diagram)*. Make 4 Block 3.

Block 3 Appliqué Diagram

Block 3 Diagram

## Quilt Assembly

1. Lay out blocks as shown in *Quilt Top Assembly Diagram*.

2. Join blocks into sections A–F as shown. For sections E and F, stitch partial seam as shown.

3. Join sections, stitching seams in numerical order, to complete quilt center. Seams 6 and 7 complete partial seams.

4. Join 1 orange print inner border and 1 teal print outer border to make 1 Border Unit. Make 4 Border Units.

5. Add border units to quilt center, mitering corners.

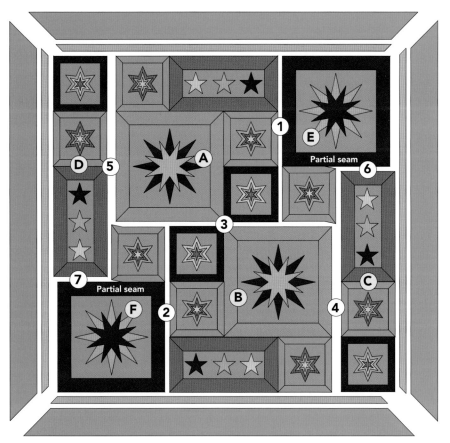

Quilt Top Assembly Diagram

Partial seam

## TRIED & TRUE

One rectangular block makes a great little wallhanging. Sarah Vedeler used colorful threads and decorative stitches for embellishment.

## Finishing

**1.** Divide backing into 2 (1⅞-yard) lengths. Cut 1 piece in half lengthwise to make 2 narrow panels. Join 1 narrow panel to each side of wider panel; press seam allowances toward narrow panels.

**2.** Layer backing, batting, and quilt top; baste. Quilt as desired. Quilt shown was quilted in the ditch around stars, blocks, and inner border, and with curvy vines and flourishes in background *(Quilting Diagram)*.

**3.** Prepare binding according to *Sew Easy: Piped Binding* on page 51 or follow instructions with Piping Hot Binding Tool.

**4.** Add binding to quilt.

Quilting Diagram

## DESIGNER

Quilt artist and teacher Sarah Vedeler combines quilting and embroidery to create stunning embroidered appliqué quilts featuring her custom digitized designs. She loves using silk fabrics and Aurifil Mako Cotton thread in colors that "make her heart sing." Sarah brings a refreshing perspective to quilting with her unique style. ✳

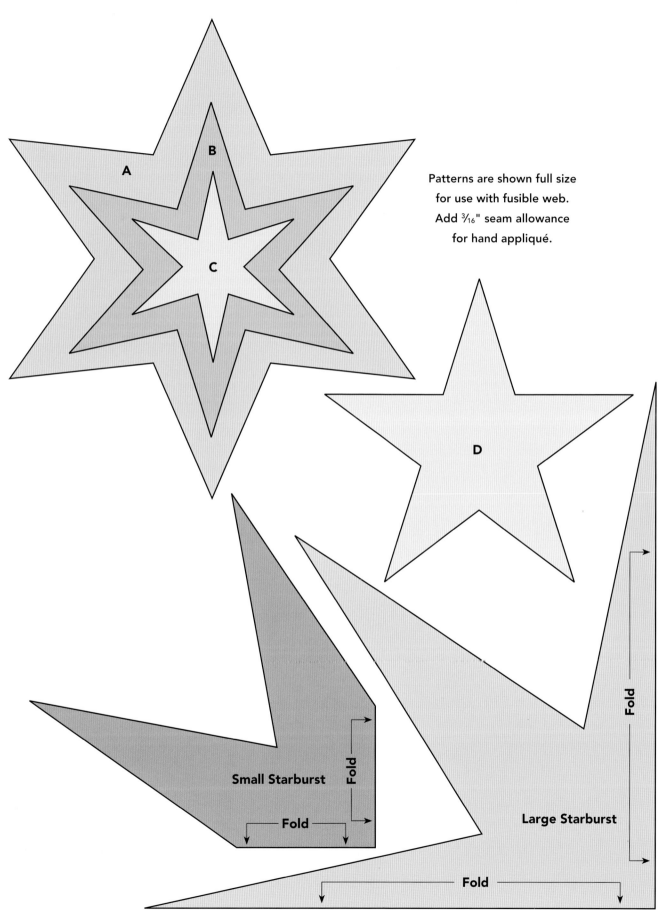

Patterns are shown full size
for use with fusible web.
Add 3/16" seam allowance
for hand appliqué.

A

B

C

D

Small Starburst

Large Starburst

Fold

Fold

Fold

Fold

# Grandmother's
## DAISY GARDEN

Jodie Davis turned tricky piecing into paper foundation piecing for her quilt. You can even piece the curved leaves on foundations! See *Sew Easy: Paper Foundation Piecing* on page 46 and *Sew Easy: Paper Foundation Piecing Curves* on page 47.

**PROJECT RATING: INTERMEDIATE**

**Size:** 54" × 78½"

**Blocks:** 12 (10" × 14⅝") Flower blocks

## MATERIALS

4¼ yards blue print for blocks, outer border, and binding

1¾ yards cream print for blocks

⅜ yard gold print for blocks

¾ yard medium green print for blocks

¾ yards light green print for sashing and inner border

1½ yards green stripe for inner border

Paper for foundation piecing

Fons & Porter 60° Pyramids ruler (Optional)

3½ yards backing fabric

Twin-size quilt batting

## Cutting

Measurements include ¼" seam allowances. Border strips are exact length needed. You may want to make them longer to allow for piecing variations. Patterns for foundation piecing are on pages 94, 95, and 97.

**NOTE:** Pieces for foundation piecing are cut over-sized.

**From blue print, cut:**

• 2 (6½"-wide) strips. From strips, cut 12 (6½") squares. Cut squares in half diagonally to make 24 half-square F triangles.

• 5 (6"-wide) strips. From strips, cut 24 (6" × 7") D rectangles for foundation piecing.

• 18 (3"-wide) strips. From strips, cut 48 (3" × 6") rectangles and 96 (3" × 4") rectangles. Referring to *Trapezoid Cutting Diagrams*, trim ends of 3" × 6" rectangles on 60° angle to make 24 B trapezoids and 24 B reversed trapezoids. Trim 3" × 4" rectangles to make 48 C trapezoids and 48 C reversed trapezoids for foundation piecing.

> **Sew Smart™**
> Use the Fons & Porter 60° Pyramids ruler to cut angles on trapezoids A, B, and C. —Jodie

Trapezoid Cutting Diagrams

- 7 (2½"-wide) strips. Piece strips to make 2 (2½" × 75") side outer borders and 2 (2½" × 54½") top and bottom outer borders.
- 8 (2¼"-wide) strips for binding.
- 4 (1⅞"-wide) strips. From strips, cut 12 (1⅞" × 10½") H rectangles.

**From cream print, cut:**
- 18 (3"-wide) strips. From strips, cut 144 (3" × 5") rectangles. Referring to *Trapezoid Cutting Diagrams*, trim rectangles to make 144 A trapezoids for foundation piecing.

**From gold print, cut:**
- 3 (3"-wide) strips. From strips, cut 24 (3" × 5") rectangles. Referring to *Trapezoid Cutting Diagrams*, trim rectangles to make 24 A trapezoids for foundation piecing.

**From medium green print, cut:**
- 3 (7"-wide) strips. From strips, cut 24 (7" × 5") E rectangles for foundation piecing.
- 2 (1"-wide) strips. From strips, cut 12 (1" × 5½") G rectangles.

**From light green print, cut:**
- 9 (2½"-wide) strips. From 2 strips, cut 2 (2½" × 38½") top and bottom inner borders. Piece remaining strips to make 4 (2½" × 59") sashing strips.

**From green stripe, cut:**
- 7 (6½"-wide) strips. Piece strips to make 2 (6½" × 63") side middle borders and 2 (6½" × 50½") top and bottom middle borders.

## Flower Unit Assembly

1. Trace or photocopy 24 Flower Segment 1, 24 Flower Segment 2, and 24 Flower Segment 3.
2. Foundation piece Flower Segments in numerical order, using trapezoid pieces A, B, and C as indicated. For detailed instructions, see *Sew Easy: Paper Foundation Piecing* on page 46.
3. Lay out 2 Flower Segment 1, 2 Flower Segment 2, and 2 Flower Segment 3 as shown in *Flower Unit Diagrams*. Join segments to complete 1 Flower Unit. Make 12 Flower Units.

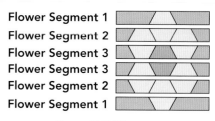

Flower Segment 1
Flower Segment 2
Flower Segment 3
Flower Segment 3
Flower Segment 2
Flower Segment 1

Flower Unit Diagrams

## Leaf Unit Assembly

1. Trace or photocopy 12 Leaf Segments and 12 Leaf Segments reversed.
2. Referring to *Sew Easy: Paper Foundation Piecing Curves* on page 47, foundation piece Leaf Segments

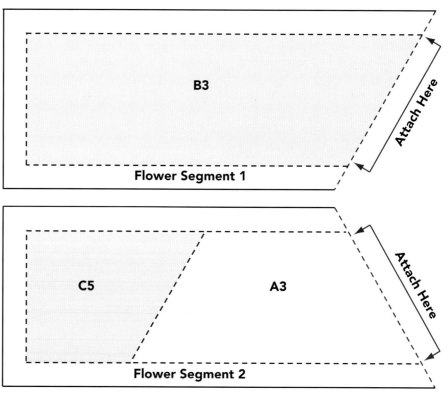

B3

Flower Segment 1

Attach Here

C5  A3

Flower Segment 2

Attach Here

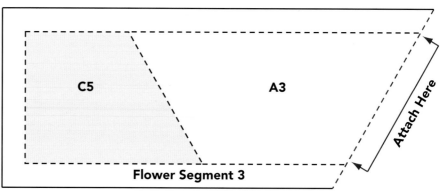

C5  A3

Flower Segment 3

Attach Here

in numerical order, using pieces D, E, and F.

3. Join 1 Leaf Segment, 1 Leaf Segment reversed, and 1 medium green print G rectangle as shown in *Leaf Unit Diagrams*. Make 12 Leaf Units.

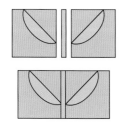

Leaf Unit Diagrams

## Block Assembly

1. Lay out 1 blue print H rectangle, 1 Flower Unit, and 1 Leaf Unit as shown in *Block Assembly Diagram*. Join to complete 1 block *(Block Diagram)*.

2. Make 12 blocks.

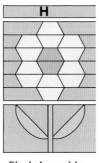

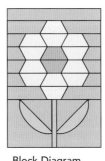

Block Assembly      Block Diagram
Diagram

## Quilt Assembly

1. Lay out blocks and sashing rectangles as shown in *Quilt Top Assembly Diagram* on page 96. Join blocks into vertical rows; join rows to complete quilt center.

2. Add light green top and bottom inner borders to quilt center.

3. Add green stripe side middle borders to quilt. Add green stripe top and bottom middle borders to quilt center.

4. Repeat for blue print outer borders.

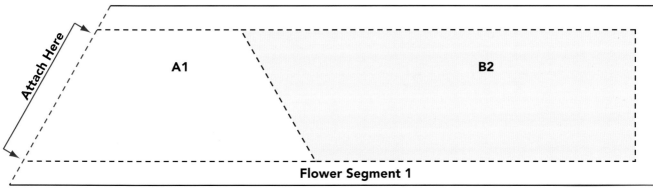

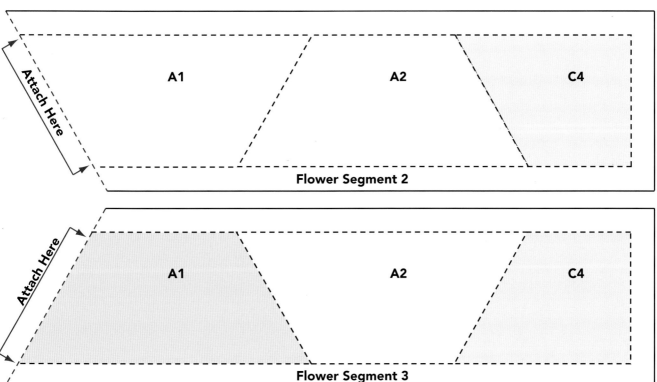

## Finishing

**1.** Divide backing into 2 (1¾-yard) lengths. Join panels lengthwise. Seam will run horizontally.

**2.** Layer backing, batting, and quilt top; baste. Quilt as desired. Quilt shown was quilted with a picket fence, watering cans, and garden gloves in middle and outer borders, and a leaf design in sashing and inner border. The blocks were outline quilted and have a Greek Key design in hexagons *(Quilting Diagram)*.

**3.** Join 2¼"-wide blue print strips into 1 continuous piece for straight-grain French-fold binding. Add binding to quilt.

**WEB** EXTRA

To download full size quilting designs for this project visit our Web site at www.FonsandPorter.com/gdgdesigns

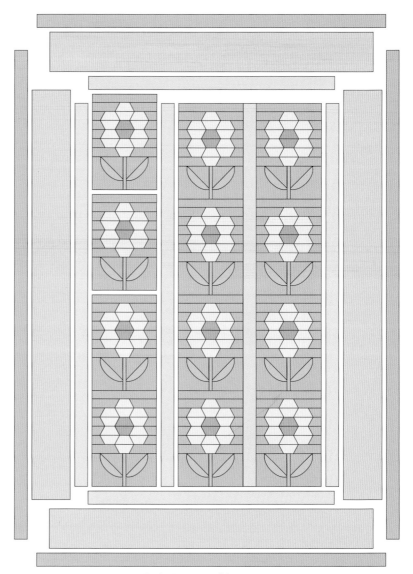

Quilt Top Assembly Diagram

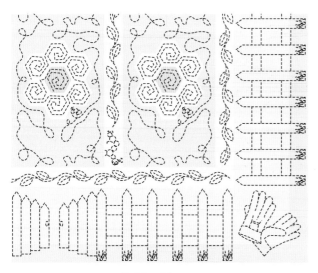

Quilting Diagram

## DESIGNER

Jodie Davis loves paper piecing. The idea for this project came to her in the middle of the night. She tried it, and it worked! Now she loves to share curved paper piecing with other quilters. Watch Jodie on QNNtv. com in "Quilt Out Loud" and "Quilt It! The Longarm Quilting Show." ✳

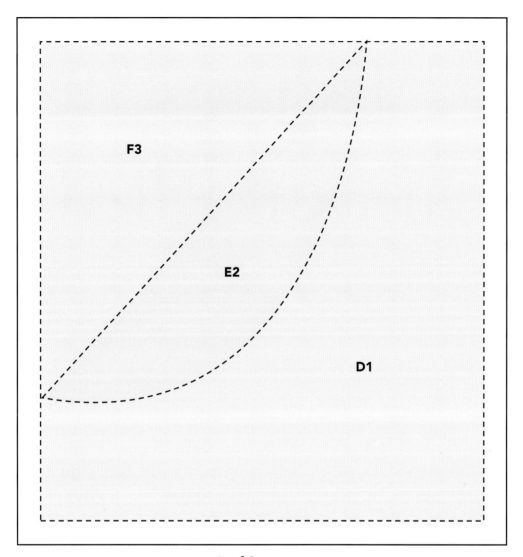

**Leaf Segment**

# TRIED & TRUE

Use a variety of batiks as we did to make this lively version of the Grandmother's Daisy block. Fabrics are from Timeless Treasures and Moda.

# Lucy's Dinner Plate

Catherine Purifoy's quilt brings to mind an old-fashioned kitchen
or a picnic outdoors under a shade tree. Use our instructions on page 52 to make
quick and easy Hourglass Units for the blocks.

**PROJECT RATING: CHALLENGING**
**Size:** 56" × 72"
**Blocks:** 12 (11⅜") Wheel of Fortune
blocks
6 (11⅜") Dresden Plate blocks

## MATERIALS

3½ yards white print
1¾ yards blue print #1
½ yard blue print #2
1⅛ yards blue floral
¾ yard dark red print
¾ yard light red print
¾ yard green print
Template material
Fons & Porter Quarter Inch Seam
Marker (optional)
3½ yards backing fabric
Twin-size quilt batting

## Cutting

Measurements include ¼" seam
allowances. Patterns for A, B, Wedge, and
Circle are on page 103.

**From white print, cut:**

• 2 (11⅞"-wide) strips. From strips,
cut 6 (11⅞") E squares.

• 2 (6⅝"-wide) strips. From strips,
cut 10 (6⅝") squares. Cut squares in
half diagonally in both directions to
make 40 quarter-square G triangles
(2 are extra).

• 4 (4½"-wide) strips. From strips,
cut 56 (4½" × 2½") I rectangles and
1 (4¼") F square.

• 1 (4¼"-wide) strip. From strip,
cut 9 (4¼") F squares.

• 5 (3⅞"-wide) strips. From strips, cut
48 (3⅞") squares. Cut 24 squares in
half diagonally in both directions to
make 96 quarter-square C triangles.

• 1 (3⅝"-wide) strip. From strip, cut
2 (3⅝") squares. Cut squares in half
diagonally to make 4 half-square H
triangles.

• 7 (2½"-wide) strips. From strips,
cut 112 (2½") J squares.

• 7 (2¼"-wide) strips for binding.

**From blue print #1, cut:**

• 3 (4¼"-wide) strips. From strips,
cut 24 (4¼") F squares.

• 5 (3⅞"-wide) strips. From strips, cut
48 (3⅞") squares. Cut 24 squares in
half diagonally in both directions to
make 96 quarter-square C triangles.

• 96 B.

**From blue print #2, cut:**

• 36 Wedges.

**From blue floral, cut:**

• 4 (4½"-wide) strips. From strips,
cut 56 (4½" × 2½") I rectangles.

• 7 (2½"-wide) strips. From strips,
cut 112 (2½") J squares.

**From dark red print, cut:**

• 36 Wedges.

• 1 (4½"-wide) strip. From strip,
cut 4 (4½") K squares.

**From light red print, cut:**

• 12 A.

**From green print, cut:**

- 3 (4⅛"-wide) strips. From strips, cut 24 (4⅛") squares. Cut squares in half diagonally to make 48 half-square D triangles.
- 6 Centers.

## Wheel of Fortune Block Assembly

**1.** Referring to *Sew Easy: Quick Hourglass Units* on page 52, make 48 Hourglass Units using 3⅞" blue print #1 and white print squares.

**2.** Join 1 Hourglass Unit, 2 blue print #1 B, and 2 white print C triangles as shown in *Short Side Unit Diagrams*. Make 48 Short Side Units.

Short Side Unit Diagrams

**3.** Join 1 Short Side Unit and 2 blue print #1 C triangles as shown in *Long Side Unit Diagrams*. Make 24 Long Side Units.

Long Side Unit Diagrams

**4.** Lay out 1 light red print A and 4 blue print #1 C triangles as shown in *Block Center Assembly Diagram*. Join to make 1 Block Center (*Block Center Diagram*). Make 12 Block Centers.

Block Center Assembly Diagram

Block Center Diagram

**5.** Lay out 1 Block Center, 2 Short Side Units, 2 Long Side Units, and 4 green print D triangles as shown in *Wheel of Fortune Block Assembly Diagram*. Join to complete 1 Wheel of Fortune block (*Wheel of Fortune Block Diagram*). Make 12 Wheel of Fortune blocks.

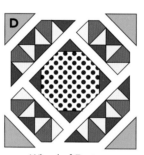

Wheel of Fortune
Block Assembly Diagram

Wheel of Fortune Block Diagram

## Dresden Plate Block Assembly

**1.** Lay out 6 blue print #2 Wedges and 6 dark red print Wedges as shown in *Dresden Plate Block Assembly Diagram*. Join to complete 1 plate. Make 6 plates.

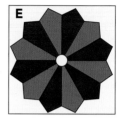

Dresden Plate Block Assembly Diagram

**2.** Press seam allowances of plate points toward wrong side.

**3.** Center 1 plate on 1 white print E square. Machine appliqué plate in place.

**4.** Position green print Center on plate; appliqué in place to complete 1 Dresden Plate block (*Dresden Plate Block Diagram*). Make 6 Dresden Plate blocks.

Dresden Plate Block Diagram

## Setting Triangle Assembly

**1.** Lay out 2 blue print #1 F squares, 1 white print F square, and 3 white print G triangles as shown in *Side Triangle Assembly Diagram*. Join to complete 1 side setting triangle (*Side Triangle Diagram*). Make 10 side setting triangles.

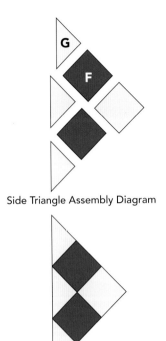

Side Triangle Assembly Diagram

Side Triangle Diagram

**2.** Lay out 1 blue print #1 F square, 2 white print G triangles, and 1 white print H triangle as shown in *Corner Triangle Assembly Diagram*. Join to complete 1 corner triangle *(Corner Triangle Diagram)*. Make 4 corner triangles.

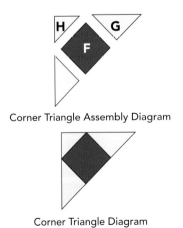

Corner Triangle Assembly Diagram

Corner Triangle Diagram

## Pieced Border Assembly

**1.** Referring to *Diagonal Seams Diagrams*, place 1 white print J square atop 1 blue floral I rectangle, right

sides facing. Stitch diagonally from corner to corner as shown. Trim ¼" beyond stitching. Press open to reveal triangle. Repeat for opposite end of rectangle to complete 1 Flying Geese Unit. Make 56 blue Flying Geese Units.

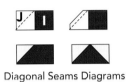

Diagonal Seams Diagrams

**2.** In the same manner, make 56 white Flying Geese Units using blue floral J squares and white print I rectangles.

**3.** Join 1 white Flying Geese Unit and 1 blue Flying Geese Unit as shown in *Border Unit Diagrams*. Make 56 Border Units.

Border Unit Diagrams

**4.** Referring to *Quilt Top Assembly Diagram*, join 16 Border Units to make 1 side border. Make 2 side borders.

**5.** In the same manner, make top border using 12 Border Units. Repeat for bottom border.

Quilt Top Assembly Diagram

## Quilt Assembly

**1.** Lay out blocks, side setting triangles, and corner triangles. Join into diagonal rows; join rows to complete quilt center.

**2.** Add pieced side borders to quilt center.

**3.** Add 1 dark red print K square to each end of pieced top and bottom borders. Add borders to quilt.

## Finishing

**1.** Divide backing into 2 (1¾-yard) lengths. Join panels lengthwise. Seam will run horizontally.

**2.** Layer backing, batting, and quilt top; baste. Quilt as desired. Quilt shown was quilted with loopy meandering *(Quilting Diagram)*.

**3.** Join 2¼"-wide white print strips into 1 continuous piece for straight-grain French-fold binding. Add binding to quilt.

Quilting Diagram

# TRIED & TRUE

We used a floral with coordinating stripes for our blocks. Fabrics shown are from the Elm Tree Quilts: The Aloha collection by Jennifer Chiaverini for Red Rooster Fabrics. ✳

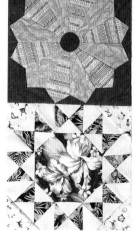

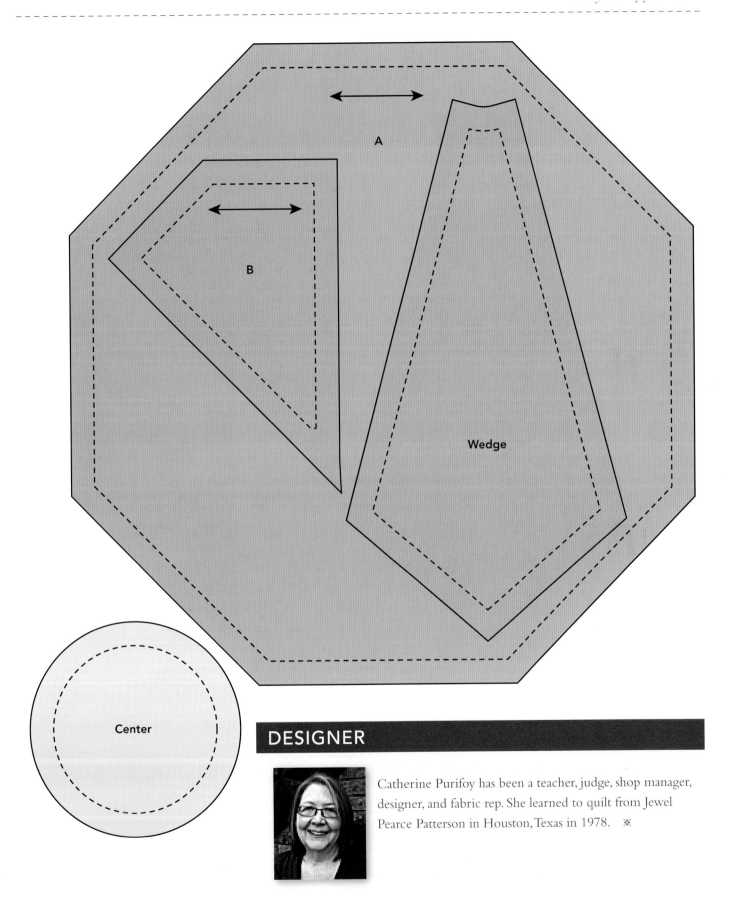

A

B

Wedge

Center

## DESIGNER

Catherine Purifoy has been a teacher, judge, shop manager, designer, and fabric rep. She learned to quilt from Jewel Pearce Patterson in Houston, Texas in 1978. ❋

QUILT BY **Liz Porter.**
MACHINE QUILTED BY **Kelly Ashton**.

# Blue Lagoon

Liz dug into her batik stash to create this big, beautiful quilt. She says, "The batiks available today are so gorgeous, picking up the strips to make the strip sets for the pieced diamonds was like eating chocolates from a candy box!"

**PROJECT RATING: INTERMEDIATE**
**Size:** 93⅜" × 90"

## MATERIALS

3 yards light blue batik for pyramids and diamonds

3¾ yards dark blue batik for triangles, diamonds, and binding

¼ yard (9" × 40") each of 25 assorted batiks for pieced diamonds

Fons & Porter 60° Pyramids Ruler (optional)

Fons & Porter 60° Diamonds Ruler (optional)

Rotary cutting ruler with 60-degree angle lines

8¼ yards backing fabric

King-size quilt batting

## Cutting

Measurements include ¼" seam allowances. Refer to *Sew Easy: Cutting 60° Diamonds and Pyramids* on page 53 for instructions on cutting diamonds and pyramids.

**From light blue batik, cut:**

• 17 (5½"-wide) strips. From strips, cut 16 Pyramids and 72 Diamonds.

### Sew **Smart™**

If you are not using the Fons & Porter 60° Diamonds Ruler, use a regular ruler to trim end of strip at 60-degree angle. Position line on ruler that corresponds to the strip width on the angled edge. Cut along edge of ruler to make 1 diamond. Continue in this manner to cut desired number of diamonds.

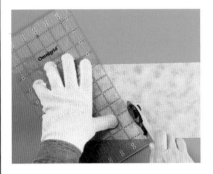

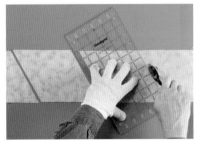

**From dark blue batik, cut:**

• 17 (5½"-wide) strips. From strips, cut 16 Pyramids and 72 Diamonds.

• 10 (2¼"-wide) strips for binding.

**From each ¼-yard piece, cut:**

• Crosswise strips ranging in width from 1¼"–2¼" for strip sets.

## Strip Set Assembly and Cutting

**1.** Referring to *Strip Set Diagram*, join strips randomly by color and width into strip sets about 6" wide. Make 25 strip sets.

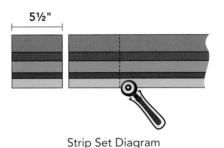

**Strip Set Diagram**

**2.** Referring to *Sew Easy: Cutting 60-Degree Diamonds and Pyramids* on page 53, cut 160 Pyramids from 15 of the strip sets.

**3.** Cut 7 (5½"-wide) segments from each of the remaining strip sets for pieced border.

## Quilt Assembly

**1.** Referring to *Quilt Top Assembly Diagram*, join 2 dark blue Pyramids, 4 dark blue diamonds, 5 light blue diamonds, and 10 strip set Pyramids to complete Row 1. Make 8 Row 1.

**2.** Lay out 2 light blue Pyramids, 4 light blue Diamonds, 5 dark blue Diamonds, and 10 strip set Pyramids. Join pieces to complete Row 2. Make 8 Row 2.

**3.** Join rows, alternating Row 1 and Row 2, to complete quilt center. Straighten sides of quilt by trimming ¼" outside the pieced diamonds.

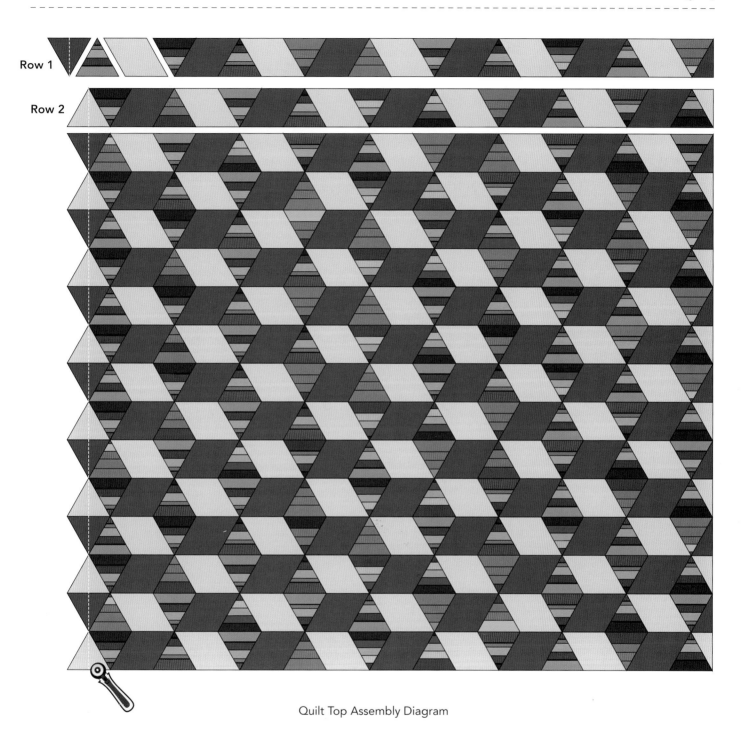

Row 1

Row 2

Quilt Top Assembly Diagram

**4.** Measure quilt length; join strip set segments to make 2 border strips this measurement. Add borders to quilt sides. Measure quilt width, including side borders; join strip set segments to make 2 border strips this measurement. Add borders to top and bottom of quilt top.

## Quilting and Finishing

**1.** Divide backing fabric into 3 (2¾-yard) pieces. Join pieces lengthwise. Seams will run horizontally.

**2.** Layer backing, batting, and quilt top; baste. Quilt as desired. Quilt shown was quilted with flowers in the light blue diamonds and border, and with a grid in the dark blue diamonds and pieced diamonds.

**3.** Join 2¼"-wide dark blue batik strips into 1 continuous piece for straight-grain French-fold binding. Add binding to quilt. ✳

QUILT DESIGNED AND MADE BY **Melanie Greseth and Joanie Holton**.

MACHINE QUILTED BY **Amy Albrecht**.

# Montana Hearth

These intricate blocks require some patience and attention to detail. *Sew Easy: Set in Seams* on page 54 will help you learn expert techniques for piecing perfect blocks.

**PROJECT RATING: CHALLENGING**

**Size:** 55" × 67"

**Blocks:** 20 (12") blocks

## MATERIALS

1⅛ yards light red print for outer border and binding

1¾ yards medium red print for blocks

1⅛ yards dark red print for blocks

1⅜ yards light gold print for blocks

⅝ yard medium gold print for blocks

⅜ yard dark gold print for inner border

3½ yards backing fabric

Twin-size quilt batting

## Cutting

Measurements include ¼" seam allowances. Border strips are exact length needed. You may want to make them longer to allow for piecing variations.

**NOTE:** Refer to *Diamond Cutting Diagrams* to cut diamonds. Cut left end of each strip at 45° angle. From strips, cut required number of (1¾"-wide) diamonds by placing 1¾" line on ruler along angled cut edge.

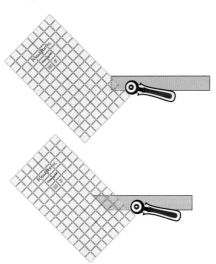

Diamond Cutting Diagrams

**From light red print, cut:**

• 7 (3"-wide) strips. Piece strips to make 2 (3" × 62½") side outer borders and 2 (3" × 55½") top and bottom outer borders.

• 7 (2¼"-wide) strips for binding.

**From medium red print, cut:**

• 6 (1¾"-wide) strips. From strips, cut 80 diamonds.

• 160 C.

**From dark red print, cut:**

• 5 (4½"-wide) strips. From strips, cut 40 (4½") squares. Cut squares in half diagonally to make 80 half-square B triangles.

• 6 (1¾"-wide) strips. From strips, cut 80 diamonds.

**From light gold print, cut:**

• 12 (3¾"-wide) strips. From strips cut 120 (3¾") squares. Cut squares in half diagonally in both directions to make 480 quarter-square A triangles.

**From medium gold print, cut:**

• 11 (1¾"-wide) strips. From strips, cut 160 diamonds.

**From dark gold print, cut:**

• 6 (1½"-wide) strips. Piece strips to make 2 (1½" × 60½") side inner borders and 2 (1½"× 50½") top and bottom inner borders.

## Block Assembly

Referring to *Sew Easy: Set-In Seams* on page 54, make 20 blocks.

## Quilt Assembly

**1.** Lay out blocks as shown in *Quilt Top Assembly Diagram*. Join blocks into rows; join rows to complete quilt center.

**2.** Add dark gold print side inner borders to quilt center. Add dark gold print top and bottom inner borders to quilt.

**3.** Repeat for red print outer borders.

## Finishing

**1.** Divide backing into 2 (1¾-yard) lengths. Join panels lengthwise. Seam will run horizontally.

**2.** Layer backing, batting, and quilt top; baste. Quilt as desired. Quilt shown was quilted in the ditch in star unit and inner border and with freehand quilting designs *(Quilting Diagram)*.

**3.** Join 2¼"-wide red print strips into 1 continuous piece for straight-grain French-fold binding. Add binding to quilt.

Quilt Top Assembly Diagram

Quilting Diagram

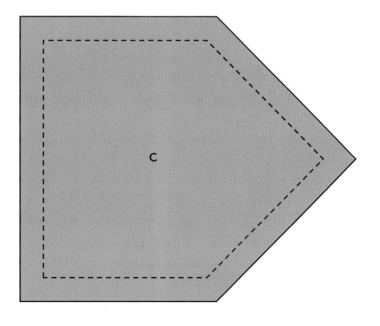

C

## DESIGNERS

Sisters Joanie Holton and Melanie Greseth grew up in the small Minesota town of Brandon. They design and sew samples to highlight the newest fabric lines for a variety of textile companies throughout the United States. Their business, Tailormade by Design, has provided them the opportunuity to do what they love and work with fabulous people every day. ✳

# TRIED & TRUE

We used a combination of prints in the Hearthstone and Itsy Bits collections by Andover Fabrics to create our block.

# Pick-Up Sticks

This quilt is a great project for using those 5" charm squares you've been collecting—we know you have them!

PROJECT RATING: EASY
**Size:** 71" × 89"
**Blocks:** 221 (4½") blocks

## MATERIALS

221 (5") squares assorted prints in brown, tan, red, rust, purple, gray, and blue for blocks
3¼ yards brown print for blocks, border, and binding
7 fat eighths★ assorted light tan prints for inner border
Fons & Porter Quarter Inch Seam Marker (optional)
5½ yards backing fabric
Twin-size quilt batting
★fat eighth = 9" × 18"

## Cutting

Measurements include ¼" seam allowances. Border strips are exact length needed. You may want to make them longer to allow for piecing variations.

**From each 5" square, cut:**
• 2 (2½" × 5" ) A rectangles.

**From brown print, cut:**
• 6 (5"-wide) strips. From strips, cut 221 (5" × 1") B rectangles.
• 8 (4½"-wide) strips. Piece strips to make 2 (4½" × 81½") side outer borders and 2 (4½" × 71½") top and bottom borders.
• 6 (3⅛"-wide) strips. From strips, cut 62 (3⅛") squares.
• 9 (2¼"-wide) strips for binding.

**From each light tan print fat eighth, cut:**
• 2 (3⅛"-wide) strips. From strips, cut 9 (3⅛") squares.

## Block Assembly

**1.** Lay out 2 matching A rectangles and 1 brown print B rectangle as shown in *Block Assembly Diagram*. Join pieces to complete 1 block *(Block Diagram)*.
**2.** Make 221 blocks.

Block Assembly Diagram

Block Diagram

## Border Assembly

**1.** Referring to *Sew Easy: Quick Triangle-Squares* on page 56, make 124 triangle-squares using 3⅛" brown print and light tan print squares *(Triangle-Square Diagram)*.

Triangle-Square Diagram

**2.** Referring to *Quilt Top Assembly Diagram* on page 114, join 34 triangle-squares as shown to make 1 side inner border. Make 2 pieced side inner borders.
**3.** In the same manner, make pieced top inner border using 28 triangle-squares. Repeat for pieced bottom inner border.

## Quilt Assembly

**1.** Lay out blocks as shown in *Quilt Top Assembly Diagram*.

**2.** Join blocks into rows; join rows to complete quilt center.

**3.** Add pieced side inner borders to quilt center. Add pieced top and bottom inner borders to quilt.

**4.** Repeat for brown print outer borders.

## Finishing

**1.** Divide backing into 2 (2¾-yard) lengths. Cut 1 piece in half lengthwise to make 2 narrow panels. Join 1 narrow panel to each side of wider panel; press seam allowances toward narrow panels.

**2.** Layer backing, batting, and quilt top; baste. Quilt as desired. Quilt shown was quilted with an allover design in quilt center and feathers in outer border *(Quilting Diagram)*.

**3.** Join 2¼"-wide brown print strips into 1 continuous piece for straight-grain French-fold binding. Add binding to quilt. ✳

Quilting Diagram

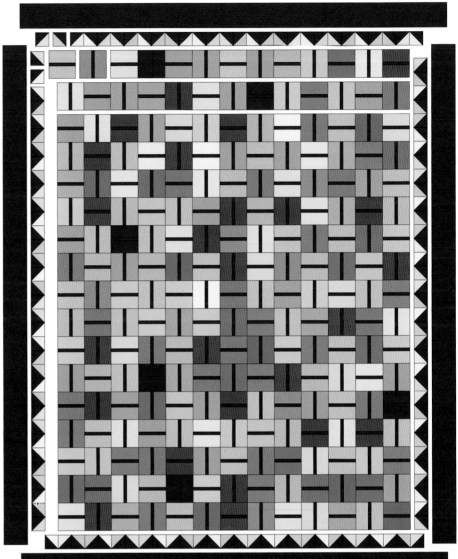

Quilt Top Assembly Diagram

## DESIGNERS

Bev Getschel fell in love with quilting in 2003, after having sewn all her life. She is the winner of several awards, and is regularly published in quilting magazines.

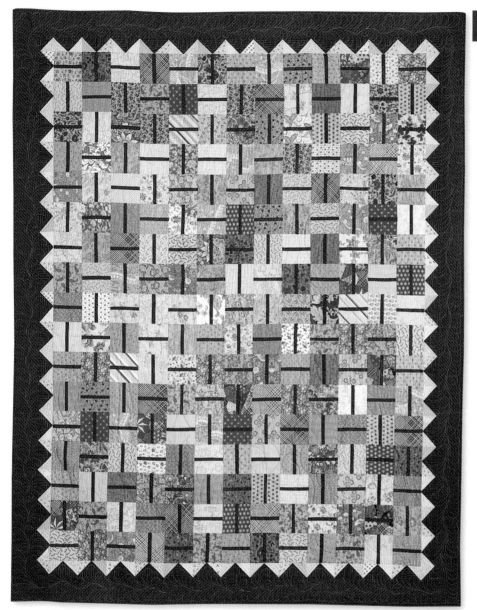

## SIZE OPTIONS

| | Crib (39½" × 44") |
| --- | --- |
| **Blocks** | 42 |
| **Setting** | 6 × 7 |

## MATERIALS

| | |
| --- | --- |
| **5" squares** | 42 |
| **Dark Print** | 1⅜ yards |
| **Light Print** | 4 fat eighths |
| **Backing Fabric** | 1⅜ yards |
| **Batting** | Crib-Size |

## Crib-Size Cutting

**From each 5" square, cut:**

• 2 (2½" × 5" ) A rectangles.

**From dark print, cut:**

• 6 (1"-wide) strips. From strips, cut 42 (1" × 5") B rectangles.

• 4 (4½"-wide) strips. From strips, cut 2 (4½" × 36½") side outer borders and 2 (4½" × 40") top and bottom borders.

• 3 (3⅛"-wide) strips. From strips, cut 28 (3⅛") squares.

  **NOTE:** If not using the Fons & Porter Quarter Inch Seam Marker, cut squares in half diagonally to make 56 half-square C triangles.

• 5 (2¼"-wide) strips for binding.

**From each light print fat eighth, cut:**

• 2 (3⅛"-wide) strips. From strips, cut 7 (3⅛") squares.

  **NOTE:** If not using the Fons & Porter Quarter Inch Seam Marker, cut squares in half diagonally to make 14 half-square C triangles.

Crib Size Diagram

QUILT DESIGNED BY **Sue Linam**.
PIECED AND QUILTED BY **Kim Doan**.

# Graphix

We fell in love with this quilt that features a mix of stripes, dots, and checks in bold colors.
A candy cane binding provides the perfect finishing touch.

PROJECT RATING: INTERMEDIATE
**Size:** 52" × 65"
**Blocks:** 80 (6½") Fan blocks

## MATERIALS

½ yard each of 14 assorted bright dot prints

6 fat quarters★ assorted bright dot prints

14 fat quarters★ assorted bright check prints

½ yard each of 5 assorted bright stripes

9 fat quarters★ assorted bright stripes

3¼ yards backing fabric

Twin-size quilt batting

★fat quarter = 18" × 20"

## Cutting

Measurements include ¼" seam allowances. Patterns for templates are on page 119.

For additonal instructions on sewing curved seams see *Sew Easy: Sewing Curved Seams* on page 57.

**From each of 8 (½-yard) dot prints, cut:**

• 2 (7"-wide) strips. From strips, cut 6 (7") squares. Place cut-away template and quarter circle template atop each square, aligning straight edges; cut along curved edges (*Background Cutting Diagram*).

• 6 Wedges.

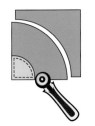

Background Cutting Diagram

**From each of 6 (½-yard) dot prints, cut:**

• 2 (7"-wide) strips. From strips, cut 6 (7") squares. Place cut-away template and quarter circle template atop each square, aligning straight edges; cut along curved edges (*Background Cutting Diagram*).

**From each dot print fat quarter, cut:**

• 6 Wedges.

**From each check print fat quarter, cut:**

• 6 Wedges.

**From each stripe ½-yard, cut:**

• 2 (2¼"-wide) **bias** strips for binding.

• 6 Wedges.

**From each stripe fat quarter, cut:**

• 6 Wedges.

## Block Assembly

**1.** Select 1 set of 3 similar-color wedges: 1 check, 1 dot, and 1 stripe; 1 background piece, and 1 quarter circle.

**2.** Join wedges as shown in *Arc Assembly Diagrams*.

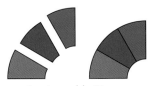

Arc Assembly Diagrams

**3.** Lay out arc, background piece, and quarter circle as shown in *Block Assembly Diagram*. Join to complete 1 Fan block (*Block Diagram*). In the same manner, make 14 sets of 6 matching blocks. (4 blocks are extra)

Block Assembly Diagram

Block Diagram

## Quilt Assembly

1. Lay out blocks as shown in photo on page 117 and *Quilt Top Assembly Diagram*.

2. Join into rows; join rows to complete quilt top.

## Finishing

1. Divide backing into 2 (1⅝-yard) lengths. Join panels lengthwise. Seam will run horizontally.

2. Layer backing, batting, and quilt top; baste. Quilt as desired. Quilt shown was quilted with allover loops and squiggles *(Quilting Diagram)*.

3. Join 2¼"-wide assorted stripes into 1 continuous piece for French-fold binding. Add binding to quilt.

---

### Sew **Smart**™

Instead of mitering the binding corners, gently round the corners of quilt sandwich before adding binding.

---

## DESIGNER

Sue Linam resides in Parkville, Missouri with her family. She began sewing at an early age. As the Head Stylist at Fabri-Quilt, Inc./Paintbrush Studio, she is able to express her love of color and design through quilts. ✳

Quilt Top Assembly Diagram

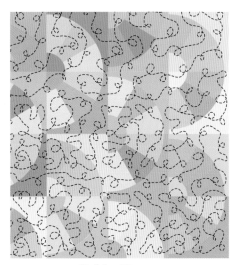

Quilting Diagram

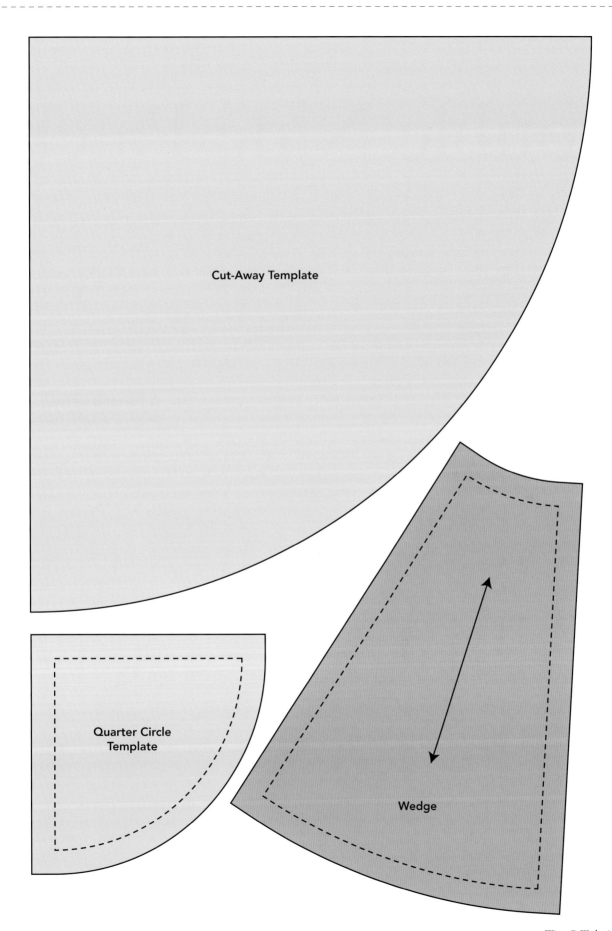

Cut-Away Template

Quarter Circle
Template

Wedge

# Double Nine Patch

**66** A few friends and I gathered together several wintry evenings, and made hundreds of little Nine Patch blocks using fabrics from my extensive stash. Then, we divided the blocks, and each made a quilt using a different layout. I chose a very traditional Double Nine Patch block with bubblegum pink and used an indigo print for my sashing. – Liz **99**

**PROJECT RATING: EASY**
**Size:** 75" × 87"
**Blocks:** 42 (9") blocks

## MATERIALS

12 fat quarters★ assorted medium/
dark prints
**NOTE:** Use more fabrics for greater
variety.
9 fat quarters★ assorted light prints
2¼ yards pink print for blocks and
binding
2½ yards blue print for sashing
5½ yards backing fabric
Full-size quilt batting
★fat quarter = 18" × 20"

## Cutting

Measurements include ¼" seam
allowances.
**From assorted medium/dark print fat
quarters, cut a total of:**
• 123 (1½"-wide) strips for strip sets.
**From assorted light print fat
quarters, cut a total of:**
• 99 (1½"-wide) strips for strip sets.
**From pink print, cut:**
• 16 (3½"-wide) strips. From strips, cut
168 (3½") squares.
• 9 (2¼"-wide) strips for binding.
**From blue print, cut:**
• 9 (9½"-wide) strips. From strips, cut
97 (9½" × 3½") sashing rectangles.

## Nine Patch Unit Assembly

**1.** Referring to *Sew Easy: Strip Sets*
on page 58, join 2 medium/dark
print strips and 1 light print strip to
make 1 Strip Set #1 *(Strip Set #1
Diagram).* Make 49 Strip Set #1.
From strip sets, cut 532 (1½"-wide)
#1 segments.

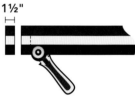

1½"
**Strip Set #1 Diagram**

**2.** Join 2 light print strips and 1
medium/dark print strip as shown in
*Strip Set #2 Diagram.* Make 25 Strip
Set #2. From strip sets, cut 266 (1½"-
wide) #2 segments.

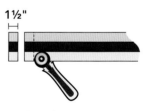

1½"
**Strip Set #2 Diagram**

**3.** Join 2 #1 segments and 1 #2
segment as shown in *Nine Patch Unit
Diagrams* on page 122. Make 266
Nine Patch Units.

#1
#2
#1

Nine Patch Unit Diagrams

## Block Assembly

**1.** Lay out 5 Nine Patch Units and 4
pink print squares as shown in *Block
Assembly Diagram*. Join into rows;
join rows to complete 1 Double
Nine Patch block *(Block Diagram)*.

**2.** Make 42 blocks.

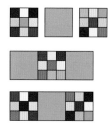

Block Assembly Diagram

Block Diagram

## Quilt Assembly

**1.** Lay out blocks, blue print sashing
rectangles, and remaining Nine Patch
Units as shown in *Quilt Top Assembly
Diagram*.

**2.** Join into rows; join rows to complete
quilt top.

## Finishing

**1.** Divide backing into 2 (2¾-yard)
lengths. Cut 1 piece in half lengthwise to make 2 narrow panels. Join
1 narrow panel to each side of wider
panel; press seam allowances toward
narrow panels.

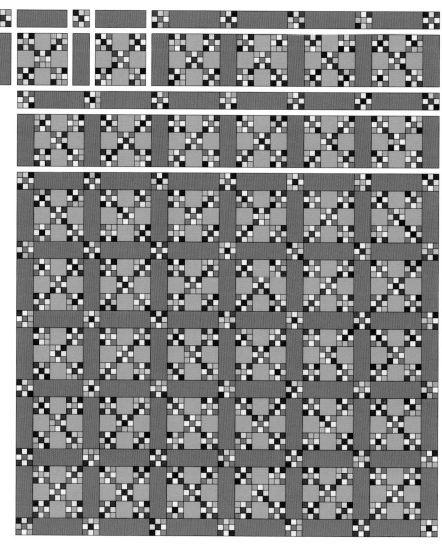

Quilt Top Assembly Diagram

**2.** Layer backing, batting, and quilt top;
baste. Quilt as desired. Quilt shown
was quilted in the ditch,
with a heart in each pink square,
and with a cable design in sashing
rectangles *(Quilting Diagram)*.

**3.** Join 2¼"-wide pink print strips into
1 continuous piece for straight-grain
French-fold binding. Add binding to
quilt.

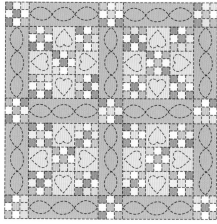

Quilting Diagram

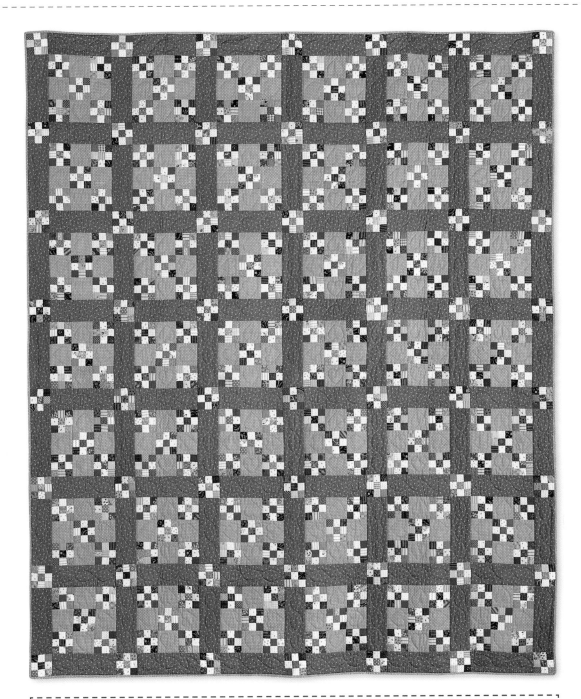

# TRIED & TRUE

For an updated version of this traditional
design, we used bright pastel prints
from the Mod Garden collection by
Ro Gregg for Northcott. ✳

# Luminosity Stars

Quilt artist Jeri Riggs created this attractive wall quilt of kaleidoscopic hexagons as a way to play with the infinite motif combinations in the fabrics she chose.

**PROJECT RATING: CHALLENGING**

**Size:** 47½" × 45½"

**Blocks:** 23 (9½") Hexagon Star blocks

## MATERIALS

¾ yard each of 7 assorted "busy" motif fabrics for star point diamonds

¼ yard each of 11 assorted "quiet" fabrics for star edge diamonds

½ yard each of 2 fabrics for border pieces and binding

Template material

3 yards backing fabric

Twin-size batting

## Cutting

Make templates for diamond and border piece from patterns on page 127. Make holes in templates at points indicated by dots on patterns. Measurements include ¼" seam allowances.

**NOTE:** Refer to *Sew Easy: Mirror Images* on page 59 for tips and techniques for cutting identical diamonds.

**From each star point fabric, cut:**

• 4 sets of 6 star point diamonds. (Position template on a specific motif and cut 1 diamond. Cut 5 additional identical diamonds.)

**From each edge diamond fabric, cut:**

• 2 (2⅞"-wide) strips. From strips, cut 18 diamonds, using diamond template.

**From each border fabric, cut:**

• 6 border pieces.

• 3 (2¼"-wide) strips for binding.

## Block Assembly

**1.** For each Hexagon Star block, choose 6 matching star point diamonds and 6 matching edge diamonds.

**2.** On each diamond and border piece, mark dots through holes in templates.

**3.** Referring to *Star Point Unit Diagrams*, join 3 matching star point diamonds, stitching from dot to dot. Backstitch at dots, leaving seam allowance free beyond dots. In the same manner, set 2 edge diamonds into openings between star points to complete 1 Star Point Unit. Make 2 Star Point Units.

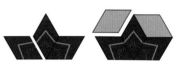

Star Point Unit Diagrams

**4.** Lay out 2 Star Point Units and 2 edge diamonds as shown in *Block Assembly Diagram*. Join Star Point Units; set edge diamonds into openings between star points to complete 1 Hexagon Star block (*Block Diagram*). Make 23 blocks.

Block Assembly          Block Diagram
Diagram

**5.** For each Half Star, choose 3 matching star point diamonds and 4 matching edge diamonds. Mark dots on diamonds.

**6.** Referring to *Half Star Diagram* on page 126, join 3 matching star point diamonds, leaving seam allowance free beyond dots. Set 2 edge diamonds into openings between star points. Join 1 edge diamond to each outside edge of star point unit.

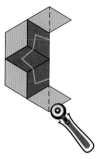

Half Star Diagram

**7.** Trim edge diamonds as shown to complete 1 Half Star. Make 4 Half Stars.

## Quilt Assembly

**1.** Referring to *Quilt Top Assembly Diagram*, lay out blocks, Half Stars, and border pieces. Join into diagonal rows. Join rows to complete quilt center.

**2.** Trim border pieces even with edges of quilt.

## Quilting and Finishing

**1.** Divide backing into 2 (1½-yard) lengths. Cut 1 piece in half lengthwise to make 2 narrow panels. Join 1 narrow panel to wider panel. Remaining emaining piece is extra and can be used to make a hanging sleeve.

**2.** Layer backing, batting, and quilt top; baste. Quilt as desired. Quilt shown was quilted with a small arc on both sides of each seam.

**3.** Join 3 matching 2¼"-wide binding strips into 1 continuous piece for straight-grain French-fold binding. Repeat with remaining 3 binding strips. Add binding to quilt, using each color to bind 2 sides.

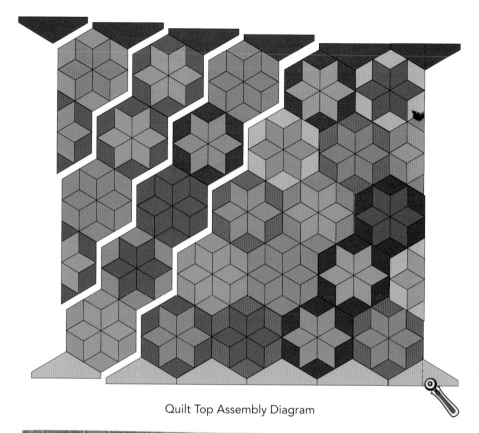

Quilt Top Assembly Diagram

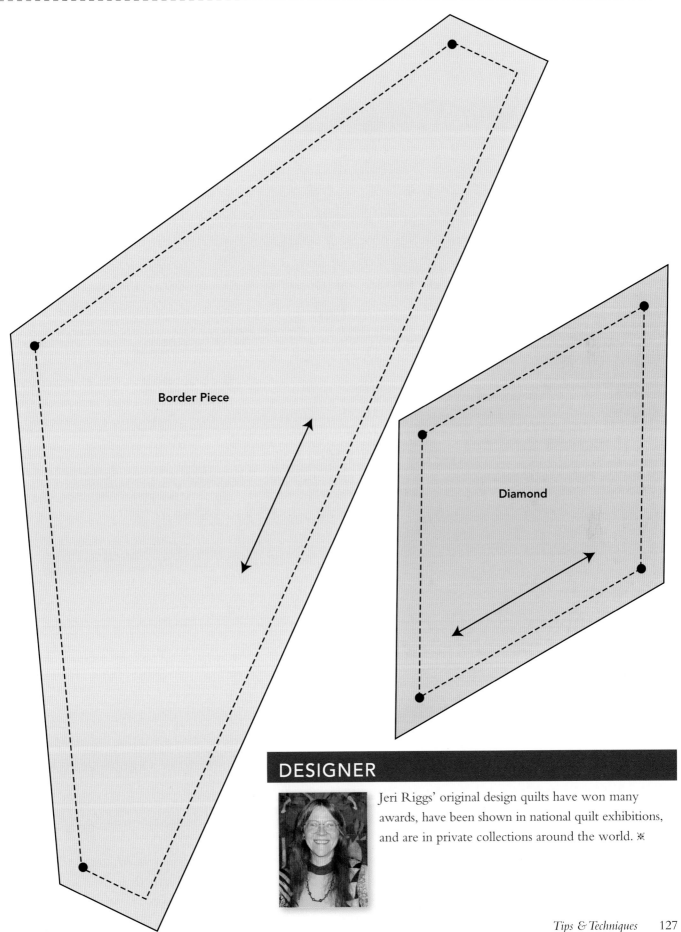

**Border Piece**

**Diamond**

## DESIGNER

Jeri Riggs' original design quilts have won many awards, have been shown in national quilt exhibitions, and are in private collections around the world. ✳

# General Instructions

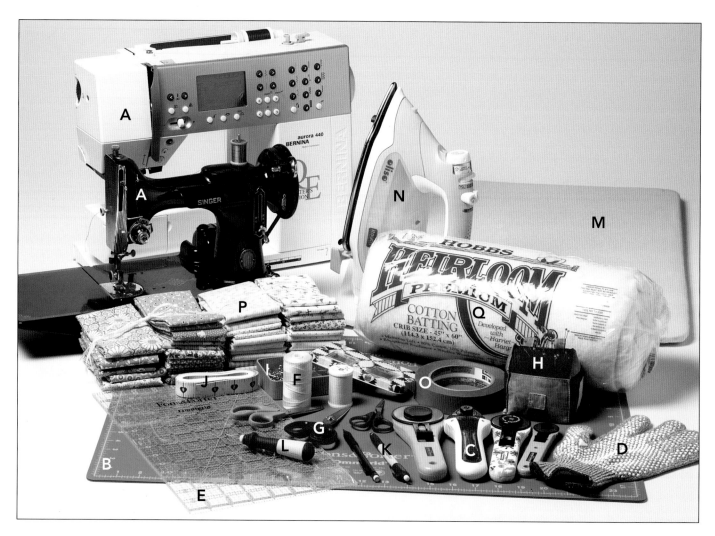

## Basic Supplies

You'll need a **sewing machine (A)** in good working order to construct patchwork blocks, join blocks together, add borders, and machine quilt. We encourage you to purchase a machine from a local dealer, who can help you with service in the future, rather than from a discount store. Another option may be to borrow a machine from a friend or family member. If the machine has not been used in a while, have it serviced by a local dealer to make sure it is in good working order. If you need an extension cord, one with a surge protector is a good idea.

A **rotary cutting mat (B)** is essential for accurate and safe rotary cutting. Purchase one that is no smaller than 18" × 24".

Rotary cutting mats are made of "self-healing" material that can be used over and over.

A **rotary cutter (C)** is a cutting tool that looks like a pizza cutter, and has a very sharp blade. We recommend starting with a standard size 45mm rotary cutter. Always lock or close your cutter when it is not in use, and keep it out of the reach of children.

A **safety glove** (also known as a *Klutz Glove)* **(D)** is also recommended. Wear your safety glove on the hand that is holding the ruler in place. Because it is made of cut-resistant material, the safety glove protects your non-cutting hand from accidents that can occur if your cutting hand slips while cutting.

An acrylic **ruler (E)** is used in combination with your cutting mat and rotary cutter. We recommend the Fons & Porter

8" × 14" ruler, but a 6" × 12" ruler is another good option. You'll need a ruler with inch, quarter-inch, and eighth-inch markings that show clearly for ease of measuring. Choose a ruler with 45-degree-angle, 30-degree-angle, and 60-degree-angle lines marked on it as well.

Since you will be using 100% cotton fabric for your quilts, use **cotton or cotton-covered polyester thread (F)** for piecing and quilting. Avoid 100% polyester thread, as it tends to snarl.

Keep a pair of small **scissors (G)** near your sewing machine for cutting threads.

Thin, good quality **straight pins (H)** are preferred by quilters. The pins included with pin cushions are normally too thick to use for piecing, so discard them. Purchase a box of nickel-plated brass **safety pins** size #1 **(I)** to use for pin-basting the layers of your quilt together for machine quilting.

Invest in a 120"-long dressmaker's **measuring tape (J)**. This will come in handy when making borders for your quilt.

A 0.7–0.9mm mechanical **pencil (K)** works well for marking on your fabric.

Invest in a quality sharp **seam ripper (L)**. Every quilter gets well-acquainted with her seam ripper!

Set up an **ironing board (M)** and **iron (N)** in your sewing area. Pressing yardage before cutting, and pressing patchwork seams as you go are both essential for quality quiltmaking. Select an iron that has steam capability.

Masking **tape (O)** or painter's tape works well to mark your sewing machine so you can sew an accurate ¼" seam. You will also use tape to hold your backing fabric taut as you prepare your quilt sandwich for machine quilting.

The most exciting item that you will need for quilting is **fabric (P)**. Quilters generally prefer 100% cotton fabrics for their quilts. This fabric is woven from cotton threads, and has a lengthwise and a crosswise grain. The term "bias" is used to describe the diagonal grain of the fabric. If you make a 45-degree angle cut through a square of cotton fabric, the cut edges will be bias edges, which are quite stretchy. As you learn more quiltmaking techniques, you'll learn how bias can work to your advantage or disadvantage.

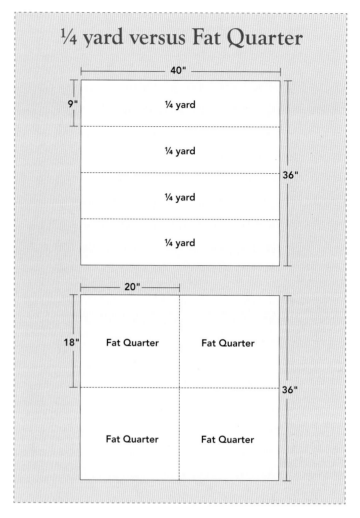

## ¼ yard versus Fat Quarter

Fabric is sold by the yard at quilt shops and fabric stores. Quilting fabric is generally about 40"–44" wide, so a yard is about 40" wide by 36" long. As you collect fabrics to build your own personal stash, you will buy yards, half yards (about 18" × 40"), quarter yards (about 9" × 40"), as well as other lengths.

Many quilt shops sell "fat quarters," a special cut favored by quilters. A fat quarter is created by cutting a half yard down the fold line into two 18" × 20" pieces (fat quarters) that are sold separately. Quilters like the nearly square shape of the fat quarter because it is more useful than the narrow regular quarter yard cut.

**Batting (Q)** is the filler between quilt top and backing that makes your quilt a quilt. It can be cotton, polyester, cotton-polyester blend, wool, silk, or other natural materials, such as bamboo or corn. Make sure the batting you buy is at least six inches wider and six inches longer than your quilt top.

## Accurate Cutting

Measuring and cutting accuracy are important for successful quilting. Measure at least twice, and cut once!

Cut strips across the fabric width unless directed otherwise.

Cutting for patchwork usually begins with cutting strips, which are then cut into smaller pieces. First, cut straight strips from a fat quarter:

1. Fold fat quarter in half with selvage edge at the top (*Photo A*).

2. Straighten edge of fabric by placing ruler atop fabric, aligning one of the lines on ruler with selvage edge of fabric (*Photo B*). Cut along right edge of ruler.

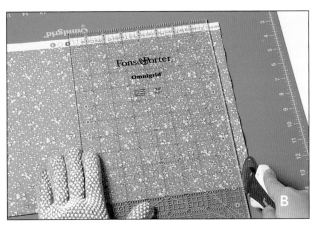

3. Rotate fabric, and use ruler to measure from cut edge to desired strip width (*Photo C*). Measurements in instructions include ¼" seam allowances.

4. After cutting the required number of strips, cut strips into squares and label them.

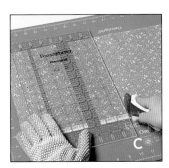

# Setting up Your Sewing Machine

## Sew Accurate ¼" Seams

Standard seam width for patchwork and quiltmaking is ¼". Some machines come with a patchwork presser foot, also known as a quarter-inch foot. If your machine doesn't have a quarter-inch foot, you may be able to purchase one from a dealer. Or, you can create a quarter-inch seam guide on your machine using masking tape or painter's tape.

Place an acrylic ruler on your sewing machine bed under the presser foot. Slowly turn handwheel until the tip of the needle barely rests atop the ruler's quarter-inch mark (*Photo A*). Make sure the lines on the ruler are parallel to the lines on the machine throat plate. Place tape on the machine bed along edge of ruler (*Photo B*).

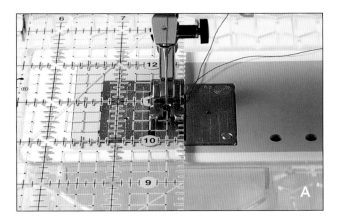

## Take a Simple Seam Test

Seam accuracy is critical to machine piecing, so take this simple test once you have your quarter-inch presser foot on your machine or have created a tape guide.

Place 2 (2½") squares right sides together, and sew with a scant ¼" seam. Open squares and finger press seam. To finger press, with right sides facing you, press the seam to one side with your fingernail. Measure across pieces, raw edge to raw edge (*Photo C*). If they measure 4½", you have passed the test! Repeat the test as needed to make sure you can confidently sew a perfect ¼" seam.

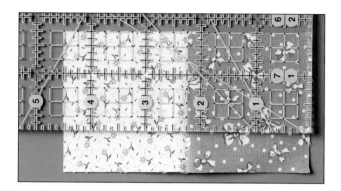

## Sewing Comfortably

Other elements that promote pleasant sewing are good lighting, a comfortable chair, background music—and chocolate! Good lighting promotes accurate sewing. The better you can see what you are working on, the better your results. A comfortable chair enables you to sew for longer periods of time. An office chair with a good back rest and adjustable height works well. Music helps keep you relaxed. Chocolate is, for many quilters, simply a necessity.

## Tips for Patchwork and Pressing

As you sew more patchwork, you'll develop your own shortcuts and favorite methods. Here are a few favored by many quilters:

● As you join patchwork units to form rows, and join rows to form blocks, press seams in opposite directions from row to row whenever possible (*Photo A*). By pressing seams one direction in the first row and the opposite direction in the next row, you will often create seam allowances that abut when rows are joined (*Photo B*). Abutting or nesting seams are ideal for forming perfectly matched corners on the right side of your quilt blocks and quilt top. Such pressing is not always possible, so don't worry if you end up with seam allowances facing the same direction as you join units.

 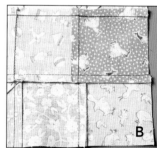

● Sew on and off a small, folded fabric square to prevent bobbin thread from bunching at throat plate (*Photo C*). You'll also save thread, which means fewer stops to wind bobbins, and fewer hanging threads to be snipped. Repeated use of the small piece of fabric gives it lots of thread "legs," so some quilters call it a spider.

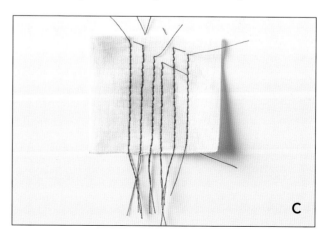

● Chain piece patchwork to reduce the amount of thread you use, and minimize the number and length of threads you need to trim from patchwork. Without cutting threads at the end of a seam, take 3–4 stitches without any fabric under the needle, creating a short thread chain approximately ⅛" long (*Photo D*). Repeat until you have a long line of pieces. Remove chain from machine, clip threads between units, and press seams.

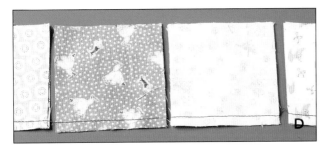

● Trim off tiny triangle tips (sometimes called dog ears) created when making triangle-square units (*Photo E*). Trimming triangles reduces bulk and makes patchwork units and blocks lie flatter. Though no one will see the back of your quilt top once it's quilted, a neat back free of dangling threads and patchwork points is the mark of a good quilter. Also, a smooth, flat quilt top is easier to quilt, whether by hand or machine.

● Careful pressing will make your patchwork neat and crisp, and will help make your finished quilt top lie flat. Ironing and pressing are two different skills. Iron fabric to remove wrinkles using a back and forth, smoothing motion. Press patchwork and quilt blocks by raising and gently lowering the iron atop your work. After sewing a patchwork unit, first press the seam with the unit closed, pressing to set, or embed, the stitching. Setting the seam this way will help produce straight, crisp seams. Open the unit and press on the right side with the seam toward the darkest fabric, being careful to not form a pleat in your seam, and carefully pressing the patchwork flat.

● Many quilters use finger pressing to open and flatten seams of small units before pressing with an iron. To finger press, open patchwork unit with right side of fabric facing you. Run your fingernail firmly along seam, making sure unit is fully open with no pleat.

● Careful use of steam in your iron will make seams and blocks crisp and flat (*Photo F*). Aggressive ironing can stretch blocks out of shape, and is a common pitfall for new quilters.

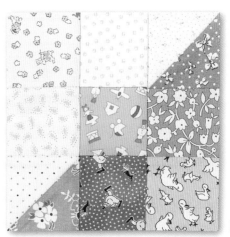

# Adding Borders

Follow these simple instructions to make borders that fit perfectly on your quilt.

1. Find the length of your quilt by measuring through the quilt center, not along the edges, since the edges may have stretched. Take 3 measurements and average them to determine the length to cut your side borders (*Diagram A*). Cut 2 side borders this length.

2. Fold border strips in half to find center. Pinch to create crease mark or place a pin at center. Fold quilt top in half crosswise to find center of side. Attach side borders to quilt center by pinning them at the ends and the center, and easing in any fullness. If quilt edge is a bit longer than border, pin and sew with border on top; if border is

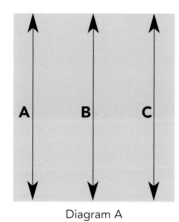

Diagram A

A _____

B _____

C _____

TOTAL _____

_____ ÷ 3

AVERAGE
LENGTH _____

### HELPFUL TIP
Use the following decimal conversions to calculate
your quilt's measurements:

| ⅛" = .125 | ⅝" = .625 |
| ¼" = .25 | ¾" = .75 |
| ⅜" = .375 | ⅞" = .875 |
| ½" = .5 | |

slightly longer than quilt top, pin and sew with border on the bottom. Machine feed dogs will ease in the fullness of the longer piece. Press seams toward borders.

3. Find the width of your quilt by measuring across the quilt and side borders (*Diagram B*). Take 3 measurements and average them to determine the length to cut your top and bottom borders. Cut 2 borders this length.

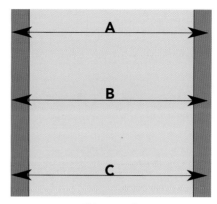

Diagram B

4. Mark centers of borders and top and bottom edges of quilt top. Attach top and bottom borders to quilt, pinnning at ends and center, and easing in any fullness (*Diagram C*). Press seams toward borders.

Diagram C

5. Gently steam press entire quilt top on one side and then the other. When pressing on wrong side, trim off any loose threads.

## Joining Border Strips

Not all quilts have borders, but they are a nice complement to a quilt top. If your border is longer than 40", you will need to join 2 or more strips to make a border the required length. You can join border strips with either a straight seam parallel to the ends of the strips (*Photo A* on page 134), or with a diagonal seam. For the diagonal seam method, place one border strip perpendicular to another strip, rights sides facing (*Photo B*). Stitch diagonally across strips as shown. Trim seam allowance to ¼". Press seam open (*Photo C*).

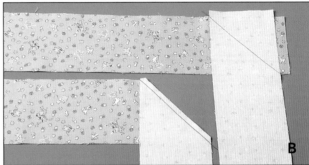

# Quilting Your Quilt

Quilters today joke that there are three ways to quilt a quilt—by hand, by machine, or by check. Some enjoy making quilt tops so much, they prefer to hire a professional machine quilter to finish their work. The Split Nine Patch baby quilt shown at left has simple machine quilting that you can do yourself.

Decide what color thread will look best on your quilt top before choosing your backing fabric. A thread color that will blend in with the quilt top is a good choice for beginners. Choose backing fabric that will blend with your thread as well. A print fabric is a good choice for hiding less-than-perfect machine quilting. The backing fabric must be at least 3"–4" larger than your quilt top on all 4 sides. For example: if your quilt top measures 44" × 44", your backing needs to be at least 50" × 50". If your quilt top is 80" × 96", then your backing fabric needs to be at least 86" × 102".

For quilt tops 36" wide or less, use a single width of fabric for the backing. Buy enough length to allow adequate margin at quilt edges, as noted above. When your quilt is wider than 36", one option is to use 60"-, 90"-, or 108"-wide fabric for the quilt backing. Because fabric selection is limited for wide fabrics, quilters generally piece the quilt backing from 44/45"-wide fabric. Plan on 40"–42" of usable fabric width when estimating how much fabric to purchase. Plan your piecing strategy to avoid having a seam along the vertical or horizontal center of the quilt.

For a quilt 37"–60" wide, a backing with horizontal seams is usually the most economical use of fabric. For example, for a quilt 50" × 70", vertical seams would require 152", or 4¼ yards, of 44/45"-wide fabric (76" + 76" = 152"). Horizontal seams would require 112", or 3¼ yards (56" + 56" = 112").

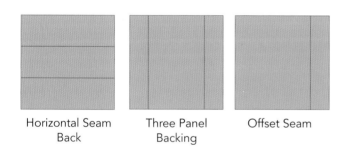

Horizontal Seam Back — Three Panel Backing — Offset Seam

For a quilt 61"–80" wide, most quilters piece a three-panel backing, with vertical seams, from two lengths of fabric. Cut one of the pieces in half lengthwise, and sew the halves to opposite sides of the wider panel. Press the seams away from the center panel.

For a quilt 81"–120" wide, you will need three lengths of fabric, plus extra margin. For example, for a quilt 108" × 108", purchase at least 342", or 9½ yards, of 44/45"-wide fabric (114" + 114" + 114" = 342").

For a three-panel backing, pin the selvage edge of the center panel to the selvage edge of the side panel, with edges aligned and right sides facing. Machine stitch with a ½" seam. Trim seam allowances to ¼", trimming off the selvages from both panels at once. Press the seam away from the center of the quilt. Repeat on other side of center panel.

For a two-panel backing, join panels in the same manner as above, and press the seam to one side.

Create a "quilt sandwich" by layering your backing, batting, and quilt top. Find the crosswise center of the backing fabric by folding it in half. Mark with a pin on each side. Lay backing down on a table or floor, wrong side up. Tape corners and edges of backing to the surface with masking or painter's tape so that backing is taut (Photo A).

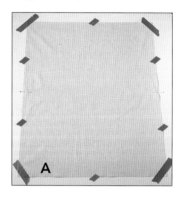

Fold batting in half crosswise and position it atop backing fabric, centering folded edge at center of backing (Photo B). Unfold batting and smooth it out atop backing (Photo C).

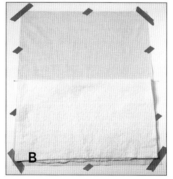
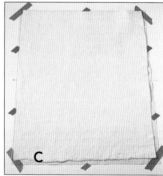

In the same manner, fold the quilt top in half crosswise and center it atop backing and batting (Photo D). Unfold top and smooth it out atop batting (Photo E).

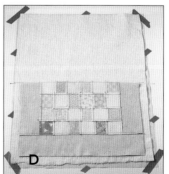

Use safety pins to pin baste the layers (*Photo F*). Pins should be about a fist width apart. A special tool, called a Kwik Klip, or a grapefruit spoon makes closing the pins easier. As you slide a pin through all three layers, slide the point of the pin into one of the tool's grooves. Push on the tool to help close the pin.

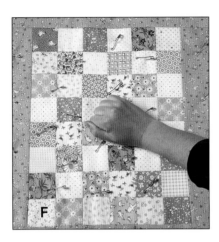

For straight line quilting, install an even feed or walking foot on your machine. This presser foot helps all three layers of your quilt move through the machine evenly without bunching.

Walking Foot          Stitching "in the ditch"

An easy way to quilt your first quilt is to stitch "in the ditch" along seam lines. No marking is needed for this type of quilting.

# Binding Your Quilt

## Preparing Binding

Strips for quilt binding may be cut either on the straight of grain or on the bias.

1. Measure the perimeter of your quilt and add approximately 24" to allow for mitered corners and finished ends.
2. Cut the number of strips necessary to achieve desired length. We like to cut binding strips 2¼" wide.
3. Join your strips with diagonal seams into 1 continuous piece (*Photo A*). Press the seams open. (See page 133 for instructions for the diagonal seams method of joining strips.)

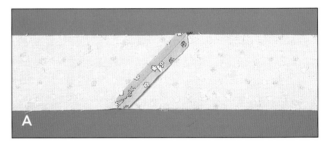

4. Press your binding in half lengthwise, with wrong sides facing, to make French-fold binding (*Photo B*).

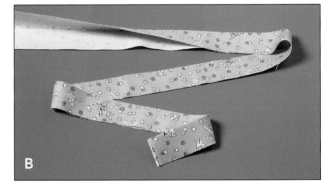

## Attaching Binding

Attach the binding to your quilt using an even-feed or walking foot. This prevents puckering when sewing through the three layers.

1. Choose beginning point along one side of quilt. Do not start at a corner. Match the two raw edges of the binding strip to the raw edge of the quilt top. The folded edge

will be free and to left of seam line (*Photo C*). Leave 12" or longer tail of binding strip dangling free from beginning point. Stitch, using ¼" seam, through all layers.

2.  For mitered corners, stop stitching ¼" from corner; backstitch, and remove quilt from sewing machine (*Photo D*). Place a pin ¼" from corner to mark where you will stop stitching.

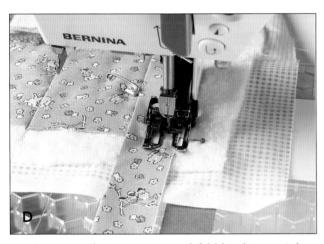

Rotate quilt quarter turn and fold binding straight up, away from corner, forming 45-degree-angle fold (*Photo E*).

Bring binding straight down in line with next edge to be sewn, leaving top fold even with raw edge of previously sewn side (*Photo F*). Begin stitching at top edge, sewing through all layers (*Photo G*).

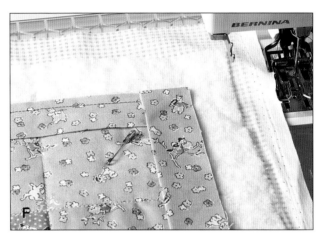

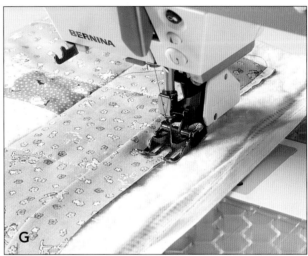

3.  To finish binding, stop stitching about 8" away from starting point, leaving about a 12" tail at end (*Photo H*). Bring beginning and end of binding to center of 8" opening and fold each back, leaving about ¼" space

between the two folds of binding (*Photo I*). (Allowing this ¼" extra space is critical, as binding tends to stretch when it is stitched to the quilt. If the folded ends meet at this point, your binding will be too long for the space after the ends are joined.) Crease folds of binding with your fingernail.

4.  Open out each edge of binding and draw line across wrong side of binding on creased fold line, as shown in *Photo J*. Draw line along lengthwise fold of binding at same spot to create an X (*Photo K*).

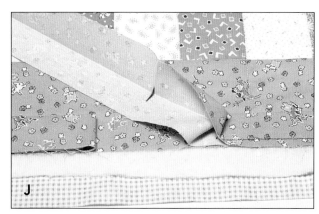

5.  With edge of ruler at marked X, line up 45-degree-angle marking on ruler with one long side of binding (*Photo L*). Draw diagonal line across binding as shown in *Photo M*.

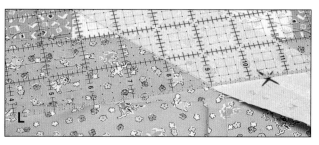

Repeat for other end of binding. Lines must angle in same direction (*Photo N*).

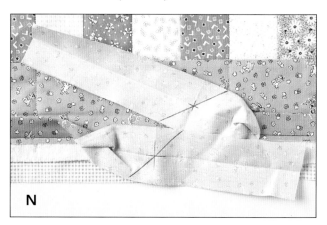

6.  Pin binding ends together with right sides facing, pin-matching diagonal lines as shown in *Photo O*. Binding ends will be at right angles to each other. Machine-stitch along diagonal line, removing pins as you stitch (*Photo P*).

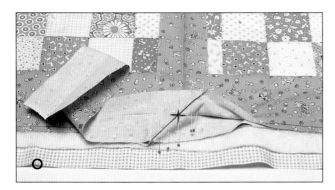

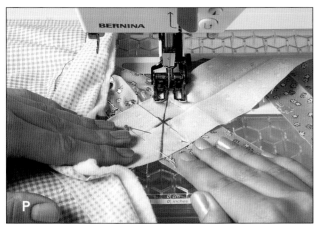

7. Lay binding against quilt to double-check that it is correct length (*Photo Q*). Trim ends of binding ¼" from diagonal seam (*Photo R*).

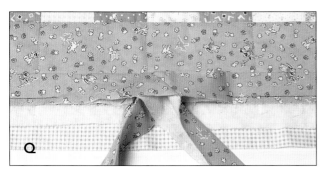

8. Finger press diagonal seam open (*Photo S*). Fold binding in half and finish stitching binding to quilt (*Photo T*).

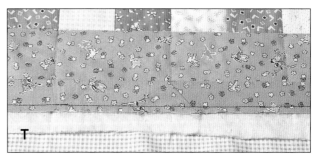

# Hand Stitching Binding to Quilt Back

1. Trim any excess batting and quilt back with scissors or a rotary cutter (*Photo A*). Leave enough batting (about ⅛" beyond quilt top) to fill binding uniformly when it is turned to quilt back.

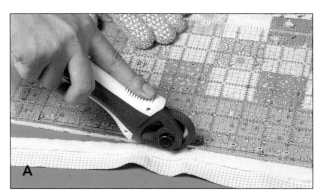

2. Bring folded edge of binding to quilt back so that it covers machine stitching. Blindstitch folded edge to quilt backing, using a few pins just ahead of stitching to hold binding in place (*Photo B*).

3. Continue stitching to corner. Fold unstitched binding from next side under, forming a 45-degree angle and a mitered corner. Stitch mitered folds on both front and back (*Photo C*).

# Finishing Touches

- **Label your quilt so the recipient and future generations know who made it.** To make a label, use a fabric marking pen to write the details on a small piece of solid color fabric (*Photo A*). To make writing easier, put pieces of masking tape on the wrong side. Remove tape after writing. Use your iron to turn under ¼" on each edge, then stitch the label to the back of your quilt using a blindstitch, taking care not to sew through to quilt top.

- **Take a photo of your quilt.** Keep your photos in an album or journal along with notes, fabric swatches, and other information about the quilts.

- **If your quilt is a gift, include care instructions.** Some quilt shops carry pre-printed care labels you can sew onto the quilt (*Photo B*). Or, make a care label using the method described above.

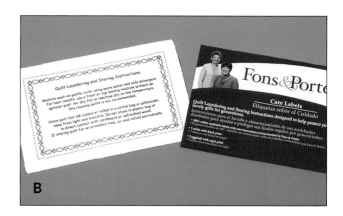

# Quilting the Quilt
## Fine Feathers

BY **Marianne Fons**

The beautiful feathered quilting designs admired on classic Amish and other antique quilts are the *crème de la crème* of quilting motifs. With a little practice, you can draw them yourself.

I still remember the day I saw a feather circle for the first time. Liz Porter and I had traveled to a quilt show near Ames, Iowa—quite an undertaking for us in 1977, when we were mothers with young children. We thought that feather circle was the most beautiful quilting design we had ever seen.

After that, we tried to put feathers on our own early quilts, but were frustrated because the patterns in books and the stencils we bought were never the right size. Eventually, we started experimenting with feathers ourselves and found out you don't have to be Amish or an artist to draw and quilt feathers. Over the next few years, we developed techniques that work every time and began teaching our methods to students in our classes for quilt guilds, shops, and at quilt conferences.

I wrote *Fine Feathers, A Quilter's Guide to Customizing Traditional Feather Quilting Designs* in 1988. I dedicated it to Liz, who was working as a quilt book editor at Meredith Corporation at the time. Published by C & T Publishing, *Fine Feathers* was designed as a workbook to use to teach yourself to customize all types of feather quilting designs—straight and undulating plumes, borders, circles, "fancies," and, ultimately, the designs you'd need for a whole cloth quilt.

I'd like to give you a brief lesson in drawing feathers yourself. You'll do a few exercises to learn the fundamentals of feather construction. After you draw some lines of straight feathers and some curving ones, I'll show you how to draw the most beloved quilting design of all time, the feather circle, any size you want.

Don't be afraid to try—Liz and I have shared these techniques and more with thousands of students with 100% success!

# Basic Feathering

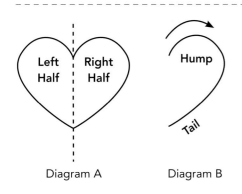

Diagram A

Diagram B

A valentine heart is a familiar shape that anyone can draw. Feather designs are made up of simple half hearts positioned on opposite sides of a center line, or vein (*Diagram A*). On one side of the vein you have left-hand sides of hearts, on the other, right-hand sides of hearts. The single, half hearts that make up feather designs have a "hump" and a "tail" (*Diagram B*).

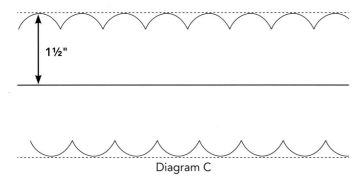

Diagram C

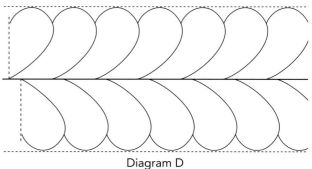

Diagram D

**Straight Feathers** On a piece of paper, draw a straight line about 3" from the top edge of the paper to make a center vein. Draw outer guidelines 1½" to each side of the center vein. Use a quarter to draw helping scallops just inside the outer guidelines on each side (*Diagram C*). Draw nice, even half circles. Offset the half circles slightly on opposite sides so the tails of your feathers won't meet at the middle. Draw right-hand sides of hearts on one side of the center vein and left-hand sides of hearts on the other side as shown (*Diagram D*). Keep the humps nicely rounded.

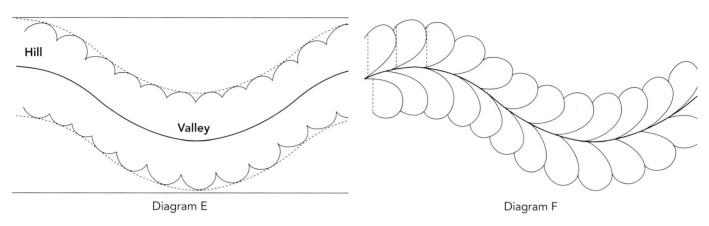

Hill

Valley

Diagram E

Diagram F

**Curving Feathers** On another piece of paper, draw a curving center vein line as shown in *Diagram E*. By eye, draw outer guidelines 1" to each side of this curved line. Use a penny to draw helping scallops just inside the outer guidelines on each side. Make sure you draw almost a half circle, not just a short arc, each time you use the penny. Complete the half hearts as shown in *Diagram F*. As you draw, be sure the tail of each heart is directly opposite the beginning of the scallop. As you feather your way along these "hills" and "valleys," the half heart tips back and forth. On the "hills" you will have plenty of room for the top humps of the hearts and the bottom tails. In the "valleys," you will have more space between one tail and the next. The smoother your center vein, the more naturally your heart tails will flow into it.

**Feather Circles** Begin by drawing a circle the outer dimension you desire. For example, if you want an 11" circle to fill a 12" setting block, first draw an 11" circle. Draw another circle within the first one for your center vein. Finally, draw a smaller circle inside the second one. The final circle is the guideline for the inner feather ring. Choose a coin to use for your helping scallops. A nickel works well for an 11" circle. Draw helping scallops just inside the outer guidelines of both rings. Feather the circle. The outer ring of feathers is like a continuous "hill." The inner ring is like a continuous "valley." Make sure the ending tail of each half heart is directly opposite the beginning of the hump. You will have many more feathers in the outer ring than in the inner one.

**Princess Feather** Fold a 10" piece of tracing paper in half both ways to make center guidelines. Open out and trace the design above on one quadrant. Rotate paper to trace design in all four quadrants. This design will fit a 12" block nicely.

> ## Sew **Smart**™
>
> For many designs, all you need to create is one quadrant. Fold paper in fourths to form center guidelines. Create the design by tracing it in each quadrant. —Marianne